PRAYERS FOR OUR TIME

A Guide to Connecting with God in Every Season of Life

Elijah M. James, Ph. D.

Copyright © 2024
All rights reserved

No part of this book may be reproduced in any form or by any electronic or mechanical means, without permission in writing from the publisher.

Canadian Cataloguing in Publication Data
James, Elijah M.
Prayers for Our Time: A Guide to Connecting with God in Every Season of Life

ISBN 978-1-0689032-3-6

EJ Publishing
663 White Hills Run
Hammonds Plains
Nova Scotia, Canada. B4B 1W7

This book is dedicated to my beloved grandchildren. Each page of this book carries a piece of my heart and my hope that it will guide you through both the calm and the storm. Your presence brings joy and meaning to my life. I love you all.

Granddad

Table of Contents

Preface 1

Acknowledgements 3

PART I INTRODUCTION 5

The Importance of Prayer in Modern Times . 7

How to Use This Book 8

CHAPTER 1 UNDERSTANDING PRAYER 11

Introduction 11
The Essence of Prayer 12
The Purpose of Prayer 13
Forms of Prayer 14
Conclusion 15
Prayer 16

CHAPTER 2 BIBLICAL FOUNDATIONS OF PRAYER 17

Introduction 17
Old Testament Examples 18
New Testament Teachings 24
The Lord's Prayer: A Model for Us 27
Conclusion 28
Prayer 28

PART II PRAYERS FOR PERSONAL GROWTH 29

CHAPTER 3 PRAYERS FOR FAITH AND TRUST 31

Introduction 31
The Importance of Faith and Trust 32
The Role of Prayer in Cultivating Faith and Trust 32
Prayers for Faith and Trust 33
Practical Ways to Incorporate Prayers for Faith and Trust 35
Conclusion 36
Prayer 37

CHAPTER 4 PRAYERS FOR WISDOM AND GUIDANCE 38

Introduction 38
The Importance of Wisdom and Guidance 39
Biblical Examples of Seeking Wisdom and Guidance .. 40
Prayers for Wisdom and Guidance 41
Practical Steps to Incorporate Prayers for Wisdom and Guidance 42
Conclusion 43
Prayer 43

CHAPTER 5 PRAYERS FOR HEALING AND RESTORATION 44

Introduction 44
Biblical Basis for Healing and Restoration 45
Prayers for Healing and Restoration 46
Biblical Examples of Healing and Restoration 47

Practical Steps to Incorporate Prayers for Healing and Restoration 48
Conclusion...50
Prayer 50

CHAPTER 6 PRAYERS FOR PEACE AND COMFORT 51

Introduction..51
The Biblical Foundation for Peace and Comfort 52
Prayers for Peace and Comfort....................................52
Biblical Examples of Seeking Peace and Comfort 54
Practical Steps to Incorporate Prayers for Peace and Comfort..55
Conclusion...56
Prayer 57

PART III PRAYERS FOR RELATIONSHIPS................................. 59

CHAPTER 7 PRAYERS FOR FAMILY............61

Introduction..61
The Importance of Praying for Family 62
Prayers for Family...63
Biblical Examples of Family Prayer 64
Practical Steps to Incorporate Family Prayer 65
Conclusion...66
Prayer 67

CHAPTER 8 PRAYERS FOR MARRIAGE 68

Introduction..68
The Significance of Praying for Marriage 69
Prayers for Marriage..70

Biblical Examples of Praying for Marriage 71
Practical Steps to Incorporate Prayer in Marriage 73
Conclusion 74
Prayer 75

CHAPTER 9 PRAYERS FOR FRIENDSHIPS . 76

Introduction 76
Prayer for Gratitude in Friendship 77
Prayer for Strengthening Bonds 77
Prayer for New Friendships 78
Prayer for Healing and Reconciliation 78
Prayer for a Friend in Need 79
Prayer for Long-Distance Friendships 79
Prayer for Friendship with Christ 80
Conclusion 80
Prayer 81

CHAPTER 10 PRAYERS FOR COMMUNITY . 82

Introduction 82
Prayer for Unity in the Community 83
Prayer for Strength and Resilience 83
Prayer for Community Leaders 84
Prayer for Peace and Harmony 84
Prayer for Service and Volunteerism 85
Prayer for Celebrating Diversity 85
Prayer for Healing and Reconciliation 86
Conclusion 86
Prayer 87

PART IV PRAYERS FOR SPECIFIC NEEDS 89

CHAPTER 11 PRAYERS FOR TIMES OF CRISIS 91
Introduction 91
Prayer for Personal Crisis 92
Prayer for Natural Disasters 92
Prayer for Health Crises 93
Prayer for Societal Unrest 93
Prayer for Financial Crisis 94
Prayer for Mental Health Crisis 94
Prayer for Global Crises 95
Conclusion 95
Prayer 96

CHAPTER 12 PRAYERS FOR THE WORKPLACE 97
Introduction 97
Prayer for Guidance in Work 98
Prayer for Workplace Relationships 98
Prayer for Strength and Endurance 99
Prayer for Integrity and Excellence 99
Prayer for Finding Purpose in Work 100
Prayer for Workplace Safety 100
Prayer for Career Growth and Opportunities 101
Conclusion 101
Prayer 102

CHAPTER 13 PRAYERS FOR FINANCIAL STABILITY 103

Introduction 103
Prayer for Financial Wisdom 104
Prayer for Provision 104
Prayer for Financial Breakthrough 105
Prayer for Contentment and Gratitude 105
Prayer for Financial Discipline 106
Prayer for Generosity 106
Prayer for Trust in God's Provision 107
Conclusion 107
Prayer 108

CHAPTER 14 PRAYERS FOR MENTAL HEALTH 109

Introduction 109
Prayer for Peace of Mind 110
Prayer for Strength in Depression 110
Prayer for Overcoming Fear 111
Prayer for Clarity and Focus 111
Prayer for Emotional Healing 112
Prayer for Managing Stress 112
Prayer for Self-Acceptance 113
Prayer for Seeking Professional Help 113
Conclusion 114
Prayer 114

PART V PRAYERS FOR SPIRITUAL LIFE 115

CHAPTER 15 PRAYERS FOR DAILY DEVOTION...117

Introduction 117
Morning Prayer for a New Day 118
Prayer for Spiritual Growth...................................... 118
Prayer for Patience and Peace 119
Prayer for Guidance and Wisdom............................ 119
Prayer for Gratitude and Contentment.................... 120
Prayer for Strength and Resilience.......................... 120
Prayer for Evening Reflection 121
Prayer for Devotional Consistency........................... 121
Conclusion... 122
Prayer 122

CHAPTER 16 PRAYERS FOR WORSHIP AND PRAISE..123

Introduction 123
Prayer of Adoration 124
Prayer of Thanksgiving... 124
Prayer of Praise in Difficult Times 125
Prayer for a Heart of Worship.................................. 125
Prayer for Corporate Worship.................................. 126
Prayer for Worship Leaders 126
Prayer for Praise in Creation 127
Prayer for Continuous Praise 127
Conclusion... 128
Prayer 128

CHAPTER 17 PRAYERS FOR CONFESSION AND REPENTANCE 129

Introduction 129
Prayer of Confession 130
Prayer for Genuine Repentance 130
Prayer for Forgiveness 131
Prayer for Strength to Resist Temptation 131
Prayer for a Humble Heart 132
Prayer for Reconciliation 132
Prayer for Inner Healing 133
Prayer for Daily Renewal 133
Conclusion 134
Prayer 134

CHAPTER 18 PRAYERS FOR SPIRITUAL WARFARE 135

Introduction 135
Prayer for Protection 136
Prayer for Strength and Courage 136
Prayer to Resist Temptation 137
Prayer for Discernment 137
Prayer for Deliverance 138
Prayer for Peace Amidst Spiritual Battles 138
Prayer for Faith and Trust 139
Prayer for Victory 139
Conclusion 140
Prayer 140

PART VI PRAYERS FOR THE WORLD 141

CHAPTER 19 PRAYERS FOR NATIONS AND LEADERS..143

Introduction 143
Prayer for National Leaders 144
Prayer for Global Peace 144
Prayer for Justice and Equality 145
Prayer for Wisdom in Governance 145
Prayer for Unity and Healing 146
Prayer for Economic Stability 146
Prayer for Environmental Stewardship 147
Prayer for Courage and Integrity 147
Conclusion 148
Prayer 148

CHAPTER 20 PRAYERS FOR THE CHURCH 149

Introduction 149
Prayer for Unity 150
Prayer for Church Leaders 150
Prayer for Spiritual Growth 151
Prayer for Outreach and Evangelism 151
Prayer for Healing and Restoration 152
Prayer for Discipleship and Mentorship 152
Prayer for Worship and Praise 153
Prayer for Service and Mission 153
Conclusion 154
Prayer 154

CHAPTER 21 PRAYERS FOR THE ENVIRONMENT 155

Introduction 155
Prayer for Environmental Stewardship 156
Prayer for Conservation Efforts 156
Prayer for Climate Action 157
Prayer for the Healing of the Earth 157
Prayer for Appreciation of Nature 158
Prayer for Sustainable Living 158
Prayer for Environmental Justice 159
Prayer for Future Generations 159
Conclusion 160
Prayer 160

CHAPTER 22 PRAYERS FOR THE PERSECUTED 161

Introduction 161
Prayer for Strength and Endurance 162
Prayer for Protection 162
Prayer for Courage and Boldness 163
Prayer for Hope and Comfort 163
Prayer for Families of the Persecuted 164
Prayer for Justice 164
Prayer for Forgiveness and Reconciliation 165
Prayer for Faith and Trust 165
Conclusion 166
Prayer 166

PART VII PRAYERS FOR SPECIAL OCCASIONS 167

CHAPTER 23 PRAYERS FOR HOLIDAYS AND CELEBRATIONS 169

Introduction 169
Prayer for Thanksgiving 170
Prayer for Christmas 170
Prayer for Easter 171
Prayer for Birthdays 171
Prayer for Anniversaries 172
Prayer for New Year's Day 172
Prayer for Graduations 173
Prayer for Weddings 173
Conclusion 174
Prayer 174

CHAPTER 24 PRAYERS FOR LIFE MILESTONES 175

Introduction 175
Prayer for a Newborn Baby 176
Prayer for Starting School 176
Prayer for Graduation 177
Prayer for a New Job 177
Prayer for Engagement 178
Prayer for Marriage 178
Prayer for Parenthood 179
Prayer for Retirement 179
Prayer for Moving to a New Home 180
Conclusion 180
Prayer 180

CHAPTER 25 PRAYERS FOR DIFFICULT TIMES 181

Introduction 181
Prayer for Strength in Illness.................................... 182
Prayer for Comfort in Loss.. 182
Prayer for Peace in Anxiety 183
Prayer for Guidance in Financial Struggles 183
Prayer for Strength in Relationships........................ 184
Prayer for Courage in Facing Challenges 184
Prayer for Patience in Waiting.................................. 185
Prayer for Comfort in Loneliness 185
Prayer for Hope in Despair 186
Prayer for Strength in Faith...................................... 186
Conclusion 187
Prayer 187

CHAPTER 26 THE TRANSFORMATIVE POWER OF PRAYER 188

Introduction 188
The Personal Transformation Through Prayer 189
Deepening Our Relationship with God..................... 189
The Impact of Intercessory Prayer 190
Prayer as a Source of Guidance and Wisdom 190
The Healing Power of Prayer 191
Prayer as a Catalyst for Change................................ 191
Conclusion 192
Prayer 192

CLOSING PRAYER 195

Preface

In a world constantly evolving with new challenges, uncertainties, and distractions, the need for prayer has never been more urgent. **"Prayers for Our Time: A Guide to Connecting with God in Every Season of Life"** is a heartfelt response to this need, offering a comprehensive collection of prayers and insights designed to support, uplift, and guide readers through every facet of their lives.

The genesis of this book lies in the deep conviction that prayer is a powerful, transformative practice that connects us to God, fortifies our spirit, and shapes our journey. Whether facing personal trials, seeking guidance, or celebrating life's milestones, prayer serves as a steadfast anchor, reminding us of God's unwavering presence and love.

This book is structured to address a wide range of prayer needs, from personal growth and relationships to specific life challenges and spiritual enrichment. Each chapter is thoughtfully crafted to provide both understanding and practical applications of prayer, drawing from biblical foundations, personal experiences, and the timeless wisdom of the Christian faith.

In **"Prayers for Our Time,"** you will find prayers for strengthening faith, seeking wisdom, healing, and finding peace in troubled times. You will explore the importance of prayer in relationships, community, and the workplace, and discover prayers tailored to specific needs such as financial stability, mental health, and times of crisis. The book also delves into the spiritual aspects of prayer, including daily devotion, worship, and spiritual warfare, and extends its reach to encompass prayers for our world, the environment, and the persecuted church.

The intention behind this book is not just to provide a resource for prayer but to inspire a deeper, more intimate relationship with God. It is an invitation to make prayer a constant, integral part of your life, bringing every joy, concern, and decision before God. Through the pages of this book, may you find the words that echo the desires of your heart and the prayers that uplift your spirit.

As you journey through this book, I encourage you to approach each prayer with an open heart and a receptive spirit. Let these prayers be a starting point, guiding you into your personal conversations with God. Allow yourself to be vulnerable, honest, and hopeful, trusting that God hears every word and responds with love and grace.

It is my prayer that **"Prayers for Our Time"** becomes a cherished companion in your spiritual walk, offering comfort, guidance, and inspiration. May it strengthen your faith, deepen your connection with God, and enrich your prayer life in ways that are both profound and lasting.

Acknowledgements

Writing **"Prayers for Our Time"** has been a deeply enriching and humbling journey, one that would not have been possible without the support, encouragement, and contributions of many individuals. I am profoundly grateful to all who have played a part in bringing this book to life.

First and foremost, I thank God for His unwavering presence, guidance, and inspiration throughout this project. Every prayer and insight in this book is a testament to His love and faithfulness.

I am deeply appreciative of my family, whose love and support have been my foundation. To my children, for your unwavering encouragement and understanding during the many hours dedicated to writing; to my grandchildren, for your patience and joy that constantly remind me of God's blessings; and to my late parents, for instilling in me the importance of faith and prayer from an early age.

A heartfelt thank you to my many dear friends, who have been a constant source of encouragement and prayer. Your feedback, prayers, and support have been invaluable throughout this process.

I am grateful to my copy editor and friend, Koren Norton, whose keen insights, dedication, and meticulous attention to detail have greatly enhanced this book. Your guidance has been instrumental in shaping **"Prayers for Our Time"** into a work that I hope will touch many lives.

Special thanks to EJ Publishing and the entire publishing team for believing in this project and providing the resources and support necessary to bring it to fruition. Your professionalism and expertise have been greatly appreciated.

To the many individuals who shared their personal stories and testimonies of prayer, thank you for your openness and willingness to contribute to this book. Your experiences have added depth and authenticity, making this work more relatable and impactful.

Lastly, to every reader of **"Prayers for Our Time,"** thank you for choosing this book. It is my prayer that it will be a source of inspiration, comfort, and strength in your prayer journey. May it help you draw closer to God and experience the transformative power of prayer in every season of your life.

With gratitude and blessings,

Elijah M. James

PART I
INTRODUCTION

PRAYERS FOR OUR TIME

The Importance of Prayer in Modern Times

In an era marked by rapid change, uncertainty, and unprecedented challenges, the practice of prayer has never been more vital. Modern life, with its relentless pace and constant demands, often leaves us feeling overwhelmed, disconnected, and searching for meaning. Prayer offers a sanctuary of peace, a moment of pause amidst the chaos, and a profound connection to the divine.

The importance of prayer in contemporary society cannot be overstated. It serves as a bridge between the temporal and the eternal, grounding us in faith while lifting our spirits toward hope and renewal. Through prayer, we find solace in times of sorrow, guidance in moments of confusion, and gratitude in seasons of joy. It is a powerful tool that shapes our inner world, fortifies our relationships, and empowers us to face life's myriad challenges with grace and resilience.

In a world where technology often distances us from authentic human connection, prayer brings us back to the core of our spiritual existence. It reminds us that we are not alone, that we are part of a larger, divine narrative that transcends the immediate and the mundane. Whether whispered in the quiet of dawn or shared in the communal spaces of worship, prayer is a timeless practice that anchors us in God's unchanging love.

How to Use This Book

"Prayers for Our Time" is designed to be a versatile and accessible companion for your spiritual journey. This collection of prayers addresses a wide range of life situations, offering words of comfort, encouragement, and praise tailored to the diverse experiences of modern living.

Here's how to make the most of this book:

Identify Your Need: The book is organized into chapters that correspond to various aspects of life, such as friendships, the workplace, financial stability, mental health, and more. Use the Table of Contents to find the chapter that aligns with your current situation or needs.

Personal Reflection: Begin each prayer session with a moment of personal reflection. Consider what is on your heart and mind, and invite God into that space. This sets the stage for a meaningful and intentional time of prayer.

Read and Reflect: Read the selected prayer slowly and thoughtfully. Let the words resonate with you, and take a moment to reflect on their meaning. If a particular phrase or sentence speaks to you, pause and meditate on it.

Customize Your Prayer: Feel free to personalize the prayers to better fit your specific circumstances. Add your own thoughts, concerns, and praises. Prayer is a deeply personal experience, and this book is a guide to help you express your unique spiritual journey.

Consistent Practice: Incorporate these prayers into your daily or weekly routine. Consistency in prayer strengthens your connection with God and builds a resilient spiritual foundation.

Share with Others: Consider sharing these prayers with friends, family, or members of your faith community. Praying together can deepen relationships and provide mutual support and encouragement.

Reflect on Growth: Periodically look back on your prayers and reflect on how your spiritual journey has evolved. Recognize the ways in which prayer has transformed your heart, mind, and life.

"Prayers for Our Time" is more than a collection of words; it is an invitation to engage deeply with the divine, to find comfort in His presence, and to experience the transformative power of prayer. May this book be a source of strength, hope, and inspiration as you navigate the complexities of modern life, always anchored in the timeless practice of prayer.

Welcome to a journey of faith, reflection, and spiritual growth. May you find in these pages the words to lift your soul and the peace that only God can provide.

PRAYERS FOR OUR TIME

CHAPTER 1
UNDERSTANDING PRAYER

At its core, prayer is communication with God.

Introduction

A good place to begin is to answer the question: What is prayer? According to the well-known evangelist, Billy Graham,

"Prayer is spiritual communication between man and God, a two-way relationship in which man should not only talk to God but also listen to Him."

Prayer is the heartbeat of the Christian faith, a vital practice that connects us with God, fosters spiritual growth and shapes our lives in profound ways. Despite its simplicity, prayer is a deep and multifaceted discipline that encompasses a range of expressions, from adoration and confession to supplication and intercession. This chapter aims to demystify prayer by exploring its essence, purpose, and various forms, laying a solid foundation for a rich and fulfilling prayer life.

The Essence of Prayer

At its core, prayer is communication with God. It is an intimate dialogue where we express our thoughts, emotions, and desires while listening for God's voice and guidance. Prayer is not confined to a specific time, place, or posture; it can happen anywhere, at any time, and in any manner. Whether spoken aloud, whispered in silence, or pondered in the heart, prayer is an act of faith that acknowledges God's presence and sovereignty.

A Relationship with God

Prayer is deeply relational. It is the means through which we build and nurture our relationship with God. Just as communication is essential in human relationships, so too is it crucial in our relationship with the divine. Through prayer, we draw closer to God, experience His love, and gain a deeper understanding of His character and will.

An Act of Faith

Prayer is an expression of faith. When we pray, we demonstrate our belief in God's existence, His power, and His willingness to intervene in our lives. Hebrews 11:6 affirms this, stating,

"And without faith it is impossible to please him, for whoever would draw near to God must believe that he exists and that he rewards those who seek him."

Prayer is a tangible way we exercise and grow our faith.

The Purpose of Prayer

Prayer serves multiple purposes in the Christian life, each contributing to our spiritual health and vitality.

Worship and Adoration

One of the primary purposes of prayer is to worship and adore God. Through prayers of adoration, we acknowledge God's greatness, express our love for Him, and honour Him for who He is. These prayers focus on God's attributes—His holiness, omnipotence, wisdom, and love. Adoration shifts our focus from ourselves to God, fostering a spirit of reverence and awe.

Confession and Repentance

Prayer also serves as a means of confession and repentance. In these prayers, we acknowledge our sins, seek God's forgiveness, and commit to turning away from wrongdoing. Confession is a vital practice for maintaining spiritual purity and a clear conscience before God. As 1 John 1:9 assures us,

"If we confess our sins, he is faithful and just to forgive us our sins and to cleanse us from all unrighteousness."

Thanksgiving

Prayers of thanksgiving express our gratitude to God for His blessings, provision, and faithfulness. Gratitude is a powerful antidote to discontent and anxiety, fostering a positive and joyful spirit. Philippians 4:6 encourages us not to be anxious:

"do not be anxious about anything, but in everything by prayer and supplication with thanksgiving let your requests be made known to God."

Supplication and Intercession

Supplication involves bringing our needs and desires before God, while intercession is praying on behalf of others. These prayers reflect our dependence on God and our trust in His provision and intervention. Through supplication and intercession, we invite God's presence and power into various situations, aligning our hearts with His compassionate and redemptive purposes.

Forms of Prayer

Prayer can take many forms, each serving a unique function in our spiritual lives.

Personal Prayer

Personal prayer is the private, intimate conversation we have with God. It can be spontaneous or structured, encompassing all forms of prayer—adoration, confession, thanksgiving, and supplication. Personal prayer is essential for cultivating a deep, personal relationship with God.

Corporate Prayer

Corporate prayer involves praying together with others, whether in a small group, church service, or community gathering. Corporate prayer fosters unity, encourages mutual support, and amplifies the collective faith of believers. Jesus highlighted the power of communal prayer in Matthew 18:20, saying,

"For where two or three are gathered in my name, there am I among them."

Liturgical Prayer

Liturgical prayer follows a set form or structure, often used in church services and religious ceremonies. These prayers, such as the Lord's Prayer, creeds, and responsive readings, connect us with the historical and global body of Christ. They provide a sense of continuity and shared faith across different cultures and generations.

Contemplative Prayer

Contemplative prayer focuses on being still and silent before God, listening for His voice and presence. It involves meditative practices such as centering prayer and silent retreats. Contemplative prayer helps us develop a deeper awareness of God's presence and a more profound sense of inner peace.

Conclusion

Understanding prayer is foundational to a vibrant and transformative spiritual life. It is a multifaceted practice that encompasses worship, confession, thanksgiving, and supplication, taking various forms from personal and corporate to liturgical and contemplative. At its heart, prayer is a relationship with God, an act of faith, and a means of aligning our lives with His will. As we grow in our understanding and practice of prayer, we draw closer to God, experience His love and power, and become more attuned to His purposes for our lives and the world.

Prayer

Heavenly Father,

We thank You for the gift of prayer, a precious means of connecting with You. As we seek to understand and deepen our prayer lives, open our hearts to Your presence and guidance. Help us to approach You with faith, humility, and reverence, trusting in Your love and sovereignty. May our prayers be a true reflection of our hearts and a powerful testament to Your grace. Transform us through our prayers, aligning our wills with Yours and drawing us closer to You each day.

In Jesus' name, we pray.

Amen.

CHAPTER 2
BIBLICAL FOUNDATIONS OF PRAYER

The Bible contains numerous examples of the power of prayer.

Introduction

The Bible is replete with examples and teachings on prayer, illustrating its significance and power throughout the history of God's people. From the heartfelt cries of the Psalms to the profound teachings of Jesus, prayer is portrayed as an essential practice for believers. This chapter explores the biblical foundations of prayer, drawing insights from key Old and New Testament passages and examining the Lord's Prayer as a model for our own prayer lives.

Old Testament Examples

The Old Testament provides numerous examples of prayer, demonstrating its central role in the lives of the faithful. These prayers reveal a range of emotions and circumstances, from joyous thanksgiving to desperate pleas for help.

Abraham's Intercession

One of the earliest examples of intercessory prayer is found in the story of Abraham. In Genesis 18, Abraham boldly intercedes for the city of Sodom, pleading with God to spare the city if righteous people are found within it. This passage highlights the power of intercessory prayer and God's willingness to engage with those who earnestly seek His intervention.

"The men turned away and went toward Sodom, but Abraham remained standing before the LORD. Then Abraham approached him and said: "Will you sweep away the righteous with the wicked? What if there are fifty righteous people in the city? Will you really sweep it away and not spare the place for the sake of the fifty righteous people in it? Far be it from you to do such a thing—to kill the righteous with the wicked, treating the righteous and the wicked alike. Far be it from you! Will not the Judge of all the earth do right?"

The LORD said, "If I find fifty righteous people in the city of Sodom, I will spare the whole place for their sake."

Then Abraham spoke up again: "Now that I have been so bold as to speak to the Lord, though I am nothing but dust and ashes, what if the number of the righteous is five less than fifty? Will you destroy the whole city for lack of five people?"

"If I find forty-five there," he said, "I will not destroy it."

Once again he spoke to him, "What if only forty are found there?"

He said, "For the sake of forty, I will not do it."

Then he said, "May the Lord not be angry, but let me speak. What if only thirty can be found there?"

He answered, "I will not do it if I find thirty there."

Abraham said, "Now that I have been so bold as to speak to the Lord, what if only twenty can be found there?"

He said, "For the sake of twenty, I will not destroy it."

Then he said, "May the Lord not be angry, but let me speak just once more. What if only ten can be found there?"

He answered, "For the sake of ten, I will not destroy it."

When the LORD had finished speaking with Abraham, he left, and Abraham returned home. **(Geneses 18:22-33, NIV).**

Moses' Plea

Moses frequently turned to God in prayer throughout his leadership of the Israelites. In Exodus 32:11-14 below, Moses intercedes on behalf of the Israelites after they sin by creating the golden calf. Moses appeals to God's mercy and covenant promises, resulting in God's decision to relent from destroying the people. This example underscores the importance of interceding for others and trusting in God's mercy.

But Moses sought the favor of the LORD his God. "LORD," he said, "why should your anger burn against your people, whom you brought out of Egypt with great power and a mighty hand? Why should the Egyptians say, 'It was with evil intent that he brought them out, to kill them in the mountains and to wipe them off the face of the earth'? Turn from your fierce anger; relent and do not bring disaster on your people. Remember your servants Abraham, Isaac and Israel, to whom you swore by your own self: 'I will make your descendants as numerous as the stars in the sky and I will give your descendants all this land I promised them, and it will be their inheritance forever.'" Then the LORD relented and did not bring on his people the disaster he had threatened. **(Exodus 32:11-14, NIV)**.

Hannah's Prayer

Hannah's heartfelt prayer below is a poignant example of personal supplication. Deeply distressed by her barrenness, Hannah pours out her soul before God, vowing to dedicate her child to His service if He grants her request. God answers her prayer, and Hannah gives birth to Samuel, who becomes a significant prophet. Hannah's prayer teaches us about the power of honest, fervent supplication and the importance of keeping our promises to God.

Once when they had finished eating and drinking in Shiloh, Hannah stood up. Now Eli the priest was sitting on his chair by the doorpost of the LORD's house. In her deep anguish Hannah prayed to the LORD, weeping bitterly. And she made a vow, saying, "LORD Almighty, if you will only look on your servant's misery and remember me, and not forget your servant but give her a son, then I will give him to the LORD for all the days of his life, and no razor will ever be used on his head."

As she kept on praying to the LORD, Eli observed her mouth. Hannah was praying in her heart, and her lips were moving but her voice was not heard. Eli thought she was drunk and said to her, "How long are you going to stay drunk? Put away your wine."

"Not so, my lord," Hannah replied, "I am a woman who is deeply troubled. I have not been drinking wine or beer; I was pouring out my soul to the LORD. Do not take your servant for a wicked woman; I have been praying here out of my great anguish and grief."

Eli answered, "Go in peace, and may the God of Israel grant you what you have asked of him."

She said, "May your servant find favor in your eyes." Then she went her way and ate something, and her face was no longer downcast.

Early the next morning they arose and worshiped before the LORD and then went back to their home at Ramah. Elkanah made love to his wife Hannah, and the LORD remembered her. So in the course of time Hannah became pregnant and gave birth to a son. She named him Samuel, [a] saying, "Because I asked the LORD for him." **(1 Samuel 1:9=20, NIV)**.

The Psalms: A Prayer Book

The Book of Psalms is often referred to as the prayer book of the Bible, containing a rich tapestry of prayers for various occasions. The Psalms express a wide range of emotions, including joy, sorrow, gratitude, and repentance. Psalms like Psalm 23 provide comfort and assurance of God's presence, while Psalm 51 offers a profound model of repentance and seeking forgiveness. The Psalms teach us that prayer can encompass all our emotions and circumstances, drawing us closer to God in every aspect of our lives.

Psalm 23 (NKJV)

The LORD is my shepherd;
I shall not [a]want.
He makes me to lie down in green pastures;
He leads me beside the still waters.
He restores my soul;
He leads me in the paths of righteousness
For His name's sake.
Yea, though I walk through the valley of the shadow of death,
I will fear no evil;
For You are with me;
Your rod and Your staff, they comfort me.
You prepare a table before me in the presence of my enemies;
You anoint my head with oil;
My cup runs over.
Surely goodness and mercy shall follow me
All the days of my life;
And I will dwell in the house of the LORD
Forever.

Psalm 51 (NKJV)

Have mercy upon me, O God,
According to Your lovingkindness;
According to the multitude of Your tender mercies,
Blot out my transgressions.
Wash me thoroughly from my iniquity,
And cleanse me from my sin.
For I acknowledge my transgressions,
And my sin is always before me.
Against You, You only, have I sinned,
And done this evil in Your sight—
That You may be found just when You speak,
And blameless when You judge.
Behold, I was brought forth in iniquity,
And in sin my mother conceived me.
Behold, You desire truth in the inward parts,
And in the hidden part You will make me to know wisdom.
Purge me with hyssop, and I shall be clean;
Wash me, and I shall be whiter than snow.
Make me hear joy and gladness,
That the bones You have broken may rejoice.
Hide Your face from my sins,
And blot out all my iniquities.
Create in me a clean heart, O God,
And renew a steadfast spirit within me.
Do not cast me away from Your presence,
And do not take Your Holy Spirit from me.
Restore to me the joy of Your salvation,
And uphold me by Your generous Spirit.
Then I will teach transgressors Your ways,
And sinners shall be converted to You.

Deliver me from the guilt of bloodshed, O God,
The God of my salvation,
And my tongue shall sing aloud of Your righteousness.
O Lord, open my lips,
And my mouth shall show forth Your praise.
For You do not desire sacrifice, or else I would give it;
You do not delight in burnt offering.
The sacrifices of God are a broken spirit,
A broken and a contrite heart—
These, O God, You will not despise.
Do good in Your good pleasure to Zion;
Build the walls of Jerusalem.
Then You shall be pleased with the sacrifices of righteousness,
With burnt offering and whole burnt offering;
Then they shall offer bulls on Your altar.

New Testament Teachings

The New Testament continues the emphasis on prayer, providing further insights and instructions for believers. The teachings of Jesus and the apostles highlight the importance, power, and practice of prayer.

Jesus' Example and Teachings

Jesus' life and ministry are marked by frequent and fervent prayer. He often withdrew to solitary places to pray, demonstrating the importance of personal communion with God (Luke 5:16). Jesus also taught extensively on prayer, emphasizing its significance and providing practical guidance.

The Lord's Prayer

The Lord's Prayer, found in Matthew 6:9-13 and Luke 11:2-4, is one of the most significant teachings on prayer in the New Testament. Jesus provides this prayer as a model, illustrating the key components of effective prayer. The Lord's Prayer includes adoration ("Our Father in heaven, hallowed be your name"), submission to God's will ("your kingdom come, your will be done"), supplication for daily needs ("give us today our daily bread"), confession and forgiveness ("forgive us our debts"), and a plea for spiritual protection ("lead us not into temptation").

Parables on Prayer

Jesus also used parables to teach about prayer, emphasizing persistence and faith. In the parable of the persistent widow (Luke 18:1-8), Jesus illustrates the importance of persistent prayer, assuring us that God hears and responds to our persistent cries. The parable of the Pharisee and the tax collector (Luke 18:9-14) contrasts self-righteousness with humility in prayer, teaching us the importance of approaching God with a humble heart.

The Early Church

The early church continued the practice of prayer, relying on it for guidance, strength, and unity. The book of Acts records numerous instances of communal and individual prayer, highlighting its central role in the life of the early believers. In Acts 2:42, we see that the early Christians devoted themselves to prayer, among other key practices. Acts 4:24-31 recounts a powerful prayer for boldness in the face of persecution, resulting in the believers being filled with the Holy Spirit and speaking the word of God boldly.

When they heard this, they raised their voices together in prayer to God. "Sovereign Lord," they said, "you made the heavens and the earth and the sea, and everything in them. You spoke by the Holy Spirit through the mouth of your servant, our father David:

"'Why do the nations rage
and the peoples plot in vain?
The kings of the earth rise up
and the rulers band together
against the Lord
and against his anointed one.

Indeed Herod and Pontius Pilate met together with the Gentiles and the people of Israel in this city to conspire against your holy servant Jesus, whom you anointed. They did what your power and will had decided beforehand should happen. Now, Lord, consider their threats and enable your servants to speak your word with great boldness. Stretch out your hand to heal and perform signs and wonders through the name of your holy servant Jesus."

After they prayed, the place where they were meeting was shaken. And they were all filled with the Holy Spirit and spoke the word of God boldly. **(Acts 4:24-31, NIV)**.

The Lord's Prayer: A Model for Us

The Lord's Prayer remains a foundational model for Christian prayer. Its structure and content provide a comprehensive guide for our own prayers, ensuring we cover essential aspects of our relationship with God and our needs.

Adoration

Beginning with adoration sets the tone for our prayers, reminding us of God's greatness and sovereignty. Recognizing God as our Father and revering His holy name establishes a foundation of worship and reverence.

Submission to God's Will

Praying for God's kingdom to come and His will to be done aligns our desires with His purposes. It reminds us to seek His will above our own and to trust in His divine plan.

Supplication for Daily Needs

Asking for our daily bread acknowledges our dependence on God for provision. It encourages us to bring our needs before Him, trusting in His faithfulness to provide.

Confession and Forgiveness

Confession is a crucial aspect of maintaining a right relationship with God. Seeking forgiveness for our sins and extending forgiveness to others foster spiritual health and relational harmony.

Spiritual Protection

Asking for protection from temptation and deliverance from evil recognize the spiritual battles we face. They underscore our need for God's guidance and strength to overcome challenges and remain faithful.

Conclusion

The biblical foundations of prayer are rich and varied, offering profound insights and guidance for our prayer lives. From the heartfelt prayers of Old Testament saints to the teachings and examples of Jesus and the early church, the Bible provides a comprehensive framework for understanding and practicing prayer. By studying and emulating these biblical examples, we can deepen our relationship with God, strengthen our faith, and experience the transformative power of prayer in every aspect of our lives.

Prayer

Heavenly Father,

We thank You for the rich heritage of prayer found in Your Word. As we seek to understand and practice prayer more deeply, help us to learn from the examples and teachings of Scripture. Guide us in our prayers, that we may adore You, submit to Your will, seek Your provision, confess our sins, and ask for Your protection with sincere hearts. May Your Word be a lamp to our feet and a light to our path as we journey in faith and prayer.

In Jesus' name, we pray.

Amen.

PART II
PRAYERS FOR PERSONAL GROWTH

CHAPTER 3
PRAYERS FOR FAITH AND TRUST

Faith and trust are the cornerstones of a vital spiritual life.

Introduction

Faith and trust are the cornerstones of a vibrant spiritual life, anchoring us in God's promises and sustaining us through trials and uncertainties. Prayer is the primary means through which we nurture and strengthen these essential qualities. This chapter explores the importance of faith and trust in our relationship with God, the role of prayer in cultivating them, and practical ways to incorporate prayers for faith and trust into our daily lives.

The Importance of Faith and Trust

Faith as the Foundation

Faith is the bedrock of our relationship with God. Hebrews 11:1 defines faith as "the assurance of things hoped for, the conviction of things not seen." It is through faith that we believe in God's existence, trust in His promises, and receive His grace. Faith is not merely intellectual assent but a deep-seated confidence in God's character and His faithfulness.

Trust as Active Reliance

While faith is believing in who God is, trust is actively relying on Him in every circumstance. Proverbs 3:5-6 exhorts us to

"Trust in the Lord with all your heart, and do not lean on your own understanding. In all your ways acknowledge him, and he will make straight your paths."

Trust involves surrendering our fears, anxieties, and uncertainties to God, believing that He will guide and provide for us.

The Role of Prayer in Cultivating Faith and Trust

Prayer is vital in developing and sustaining our faith and trust in God. Through prayer, we communicate with God, express our dependence on Him, and invite His presence and power into our lives.

Strengthening Faith Through Prayer

Prayer strengthens our faith by deepening our relationship with God. As we spend time in His presence, we grow more aware of His character, love, and faithfulness. The more we know God, the more our faith is fortified. Romans 10:17 tells us,

"So faith comes from hearing, and hearing through the word of Christ."

Praying Scripture is a powerful way to build our faith, as it reminds us of God's promises and His past faithfulness.

Building Trust Through Prayer

Prayer builds trust by helping us surrender our worries and concerns to God. Philippians 4:6-7 encourages us,

"Do not be anxious about anything, but in everything by prayer and supplication with thanksgiving let your requests be made known to God. And the peace of God, which surpasses all understanding, will guard your hearts and your minds in Christ Jesus."

When we bring our anxieties to God in prayer, we experience His peace, which strengthens our trust in His provision and care.

Prayers for Faith and Trust

Prayers of Affirmation

Affirming God's attributes and promises in prayer reinforces our faith and trust. These prayers focus on who God is and what He has promised to do.

Example: *"Heavenly Father, I affirm that You are faithful and true. Your promises never fail, and Your love endures forever. I trust in Your provision and guidance, knowing that You are my Shepherd and I shall not want. Strengthen my faith, Lord, and help me to rely on You in every situation. Amen."*

Prayers of Surrender

Prayers of surrender involve releasing our fears, anxieties, and plans to God, trusting Him to lead and provide.

Example: *"Lord, I surrender my worries and fears to You. I trust that You know what is best for me and that You are working all things for my good. Help me to rest in Your promises and to trust in Your timing. Guide my steps, Lord, and lead me in the path of Your righteousness. Amen."*

Prayers for Increased Faith

Asking God to increase our faith is a humble acknowledgment of our dependence on Him.

Example: *"Father, I believe; help my unbelief. Increase my faith, Lord, so that I may trust You more deeply and follow You more faithfully. Fill me with Your Holy Spirit, and strengthen my resolve to walk by faith and not by sight. May my faith in You grow stronger each day, and may I be a witness to Your faithfulness in all that I do. Amen."*

Prayers for Trust in Uncertainty

When facing uncertainty or difficult circumstances, prayers for trust help us rely on God's wisdom and guidance.

Example: *"God, in times of uncertainty, I choose to trust You. You are my refuge and strength, an ever-present help in trouble. Calm my anxious heart and remind me of Your sovereignty and love. Lead me with Your wisdom, and help me to trust in Your perfect plan. I place my hope and confidence in You, knowing that You are in control. Amen."*

Practical Ways to Incorporate Prayers for Faith and Trust

Daily Devotions

Incorporating prayers for faith and trust into daily devotions keeps our focus on God and strengthens our spiritual foundation. Begin and end your day with prayers that affirm God's faithfulness and express your trust in His guidance.

Scripture Meditation

Meditating on Scriptures that speak of faith and trust enriches our prayer life. Verses like Psalm 56:3, "When I am afraid, I put my trust in you," and Isaiah 26:3, "You keep him in perfect peace whose mind is stayed on you, because he trusts in you," provide a basis for powerful prayers.

Journaling Prayers

Keeping a prayer journal helps track God's faithfulness over time. Write down your prayers for faith and trust, noting how God answers and sustains you. Reviewing these entries can boost your faith and trust during challenging times.

Community Prayer

Praying with others strengthens collective faith and trust. Join a prayer group or find a prayer partner to support each other in faith and trust through communal prayer.

Conclusion

Faith and trust are essential components of a vibrant spiritual life, anchoring us in God's promises and sustaining us through all of life's challenges. Prayer is the means through which we cultivate and strengthen these qualities, drawing us closer to God and reinforcing our reliance on Him. By incorporating prayers for faith and trust into our daily lives, we grow in our relationship with God, experience His peace, and become more resilient in the face of uncertainties. As we journey in prayer, may our faith be strengthened and our trust in God deepened, leading us to a more profound experience of His love and faithfulness.

Prayer

Heavenly Father,

We come before You with hearts full of gratitude for Your unwavering faithfulness and love. Strengthen our faith, Lord, that we may trust in You more deeply and follow You more faithfully. Help us to surrender our fears and anxieties, knowing that You are our refuge and strength. Guide our steps and lead us in Your perfect wisdom. May our lives be a testament to Your faithfulness, and may we grow in faith and trust each day.

In Jesus' name, we pray.

Amen.

CHAPTER 4
PRAYERS FOR WISDOM AND GUIDANCE

True wisdom comes from God, and He is eager to guide those who seek Him.

Introduction

In a world filled with complexity and uncertainty, the need for wisdom and guidance is paramount. The Bible teaches that true wisdom comes from God and that He is eager to guide those who seek Him. This chapter delves into the importance of seeking divine wisdom and guidance through prayer, exploring biblical examples and practical steps to incorporate these prayers into our daily lives.

The Importance of Wisdom and Guidance

Defining Wisdom

Wisdom, as described in the Bible, goes beyond mere knowledge or intelligence. It encompasses understanding, discernment, and the ability to make godly decisions. Proverbs 2:6 says,

"For the Lord gives wisdom; from his mouth come knowledge and understanding."

Biblical wisdom is rooted in a reverent relationship with God and a commitment to living according to His principles.

The Need for Guidance

Guidance is essential in navigating the complexities of life. It involves seeking God's direction and aligning our paths with His will. Proverbs 3:5-6 instructs,

"Trust in the Lord with all your heart, and do not lean on your own understanding. In all your ways acknowledge him, and he will make straight your paths."

When we seek God's guidance, we invite His sovereign direction into every aspect of our lives.

Biblical Examples of Seeking Wisdom and Guidance

Solomon's Request for Wisdom

King Solomon is renowned for his wisdom, which he received from God in response to his humble request. In 1 Kings 3:5-12, Solomon asks for an understanding heart to judge God's people wisely. God grants Solomon unparalleled wisdom, which he uses to lead Israel. Solomon's example teaches us the importance of prioritizing wisdom and seeking it earnestly from God.

David's Prayers for Guidance

King David often sought God's guidance, especially in times of trouble. Psalm 25 is a heartfelt prayer for guidance and forgiveness. In verses 4-5, David prays,

"Make me to know your ways, O Lord; teach me your paths. Lead me in your truth and teach me, for you are the God of my salvation; for you I wait all the day long."

David's reliance on God for direction highlights the necessity of continual dependence on divine guidance.

The Early Church's Dependence on God's Guidance

The early church consistently sought God's wisdom and guidance, particularly in decision-making. In Acts 13:2-3, the church in Antioch fasts and prays for direction, resulting in the Holy Spirit's instruction to set apart Barnabas and Saul for missionary work. This example underscores the importance of collective prayer and fasting when seeking God's guidance.

Prayers for Wisdom and Guidance

Prayers for Personal Wisdom

Seeking personal wisdom through prayer involves asking God to impart His understanding and discernment in our lives.

Example: *"Heavenly Father, I come before You seeking Your wisdom. Grant me understanding and discernment in all my decisions. Help me to see things from Your perspective and to act according to Your will. Fill me with Your Spirit, that I may walk in Your ways and reflect Your wisdom in my actions. Amen."*

Prayers for Direction in Decision-Making

When faced with important decisions, praying for guidance invites God's direction and clarity.

Example: *"Lord, I need Your guidance as I make decisions about [specific situation]. Show me the path You want me to take and give me the courage to follow it. Help me to trust in Your plan and to listen for Your voice. Guide my thoughts and actions, and let Your will be done in my life. Amen."*

Prayers for Collective Guidance

In times of communal decision-making, praying together for God's guidance fosters unity and dependence on Him.

Example: *"Father, as we come together to seek Your guidance for [specific situation], we ask for Your wisdom and direction. Unite our hearts and minds in Your will. Help us to discern Your leading and to follow Your guidance faithfully. We trust in Your sovereign plan and commit our decisions to You. Amen."*

Practical Steps to Incorporate Prayers for Wisdom and Guidance

Regular Devotional Time

Setting aside regular time for prayer and Bible study helps us seek God's wisdom and guidance consistently. Reflect on passages such as James 1:5, which encourages us to ask God for wisdom, trusting that He gives generously to those who seek.

Fasting and Prayer

Fasting, combined with prayer, heightens our spiritual sensitivity and focus. Consider setting aside specific times for fasting and prayer when seeking God's guidance for significant decisions.

Seeking Godly Counsel

While prayer is paramount, seeking advice from godly mentors and fellow believers can provide additional insights and confirmation of God's guidance. Proverbs 11:14 reminds us,

"Where there is no guidance, a people falls, but in an abundance of counselors there is safety."

Journaling Prayers

Keeping a prayer journal allows you to document your requests for wisdom and guidance and to record how God responds. This practice not only helps you stay focused in prayer but also provides a record of God's faithfulness and direction over time.

Conclusion

Prayers for wisdom and guidance are vital for navigating life's complexities and aligning our paths with God's will. The Bible provides abundant examples and encouragement to seek divine wisdom and direction through earnest prayer. By incorporating these prayers into our daily lives, we can grow in understanding, make godly decisions, and experience the peace that comes from following God's lead. As we cultivate a habit of seeking God's wisdom and guidance, we become more attuned to His voice and more confident in His direction for our lives.

Prayer

Heavenly Father,

We thank You for Your promise to give wisdom generously to those who ask. As we seek Your guidance and direction, fill us with Your Spirit and impart Your wisdom to our hearts and minds. Help us to trust in Your perfect plan and to follow Your leading faithfully. Guide our steps, Lord, and let Your will be done in our lives. May we reflect Your wisdom in all that we do, bringing glory to Your name.

In Jesus' name, we pray.

Amen.

CHAPTER 5
PRAYERS FOR HEALING AND RESTORATION

We can always turn to God for healing and restoration.

Introduction

Healing and restoration are profound themes in the Bible, reflecting God's desire to make whole that which is broken. Whether we face physical illness, emotional wounds, or spiritual brokenness, turning to God in prayer for healing and restoration can bring comfort, strength, and renewal. This chapter explores the biblical basis for prayers of healing and restoration, offers examples of such prayers, and provides practical ways to incorporate them into our daily lives.

Biblical Basis for Healing and Restoration

God's Desire to Heal

The Bible consistently portrays God as a healer. Exodus 15:26 declares, "I am the Lord, your healer." God's healing power is evident throughout the scriptures, demonstrating His compassion and desire to restore His people. Jesus' ministry on earth was marked by numerous healings, revealing God's heart to bring wholeness to every aspect of our lives.

Healing Through Faith

Faith plays a crucial role in receiving God's healing. In the New Testament, many individuals were healed through their faith in Jesus. For instance, in Mark 5:34, Jesus says to a woman who had been healed of her bleeding,

"Daughter, your faith has made you well; go in peace, and be healed of your disease."

This example underscores the importance of faith in seeking God's healing.

The Power of Restoration

Restoration goes beyond physical healing, encompassing emotional, relational, and spiritual renewal. Psalm 23:3 states,

"He restores my soul."

God's restorative power is seen in His ability to bring new life and hope to areas of deep brokenness. Joel 2:25 further promises,

"I will restore to you the years that the swarming locust has eaten,"

highlighting God's commitment to restore what has been lost or damaged.

Prayers for Healing and Restoration

Prayers for Physical Healing

Seeking physical healing through prayer involves asking God to bring health and wholeness to our bodies.

Example: *"Heavenly Father, I come before You in need of Your healing touch. I ask for Your power to restore health to my body. Remove any illness, pain, or weakness, and strengthen me with Your healing power. I trust in Your ability to heal and Your desire to make me whole. In Jesus' name, I pray. Amen."*

Prayers for Emotional Healing

Emotional wounds can be deep and lasting, but God offers healing for our hearts and minds.

Example: *"Lord, I bring my broken heart before You, asking for Your healing and comfort. Mend the wounds that have caused pain and restore my emotional well-being. Help me to release any bitterness, anger, or sadness, and fill me with Your peace and joy. I trust in Your loving care and Your power to heal. Amen."*

Prayers for Relational Restoration

Restored relationships are a testament to God's ability to bring reconciliation and peace.

Example: *"Father, I lift up my broken relationships to You, asking for Your restoration and healing. Bring reconciliation where there has been conflict, understanding where there has been misunderstanding, and love where there has been hurt. Guide us in forgiveness and help us to rebuild trust. I trust in Your power to restore and renew. Amen."*

Prayers for Spiritual Renewal

Spiritual restoration involves seeking God's renewal in our relationship with Him.

Example: *"Lord, I come to You seeking spiritual renewal. Restore my soul and rekindle my passion for You. Remove any barriers that have hindered my relationship with You and fill me with Your Holy Spirit. Strengthen my faith and draw me closer to You each day. I trust in Your power to renew and restore my spirit. Amen."*

Biblical Examples of Healing and Restoration

The Healing of Naaman

Naaman, a commander of the Syrian army, was healed of leprosy after following the prophet Elisha's instructions to wash in the Jordan River (2 Kings 5:1-14). This story illustrates the importance of obedience and faith in receiving God's healing.

The Prodigal Son

The parable of the prodigal son (Luke 15:11-32) is a powerful example of relational and spiritual restoration. The father's unconditional love and forgiveness towards his repentant son demonstrate God's desire to restore broken relationships and bring spiritual renewal.

The Healing of the Paralyzed Man

In Mark 2:1-12, Jesus heals a paralyzed man brought to Him by four friends. This story highlights the role of community and faith in seeking healing. Jesus not only heals the man physically but also forgives his sins, showcasing the holistic nature of God's healing.

Practical Steps to Incorporate Prayers for Healing and Restoration

Regular Prayer Time

Setting aside regular time for prayer allows us to seek God's healing and restoration consistently. Create a daily routine where you can bring your physical, emotional, relational, and spiritual needs before God.

Fasting and Prayer

Fasting, combined with prayer, can intensify our focus and dependence on God. Consider fasting for a day or a specific meal while praying for healing and restoration in particular areas of your life.

Prayer Partners and Groups

Joining with others in prayer can strengthen our petitions and provide support. Find a prayer partner or join a prayer group to pray together for healing and restoration. Collective prayer can be powerful and encouraging.

Anointing and Laying on of Hands

James 5:14-15 advises,

"Is anyone among you sick? Let them call the elders of the church to pray over them and anoint them with oil in the name of the Lord. And the prayer offered in faith will make the sick person well; the Lord will raise them up."

Following this biblical practice can be a meaningful way to seek physical healing.

Meditation on Healing Scriptures

Meditating on scriptures that speak of God's healing and restoration can bolster our faith and provide comfort. Passages such as Isaiah 53:5,

"By his wounds we are healed,"

and Psalm 147:3,

"He heals the brokenhearted and binds up their wounds,"

are powerful reminders of God's promises

Conclusion

Prayers for healing and restoration tap into God's profound desire to make us whole. Whether we seek physical, emotional, relational, or spiritual healing, turning to God in prayer allows us to experience His transformative power. The Bible is filled with examples of God's healing and restorative work, encouraging us to seek Him with faith and trust. By incorporating these prayers into our daily lives, we open ourselves to the healing and restoration that God longs to provide. May we continually seek His touch, trusting in His love and power to make us whole.

Prayer

Heavenly Father,

We thank You for Your unwavering love and Your desire to heal and restore us. We come before You, asking for Your healing touch in every area of our lives. Restore our bodies, heal our hearts, mend our relationships, and renew our spirits. Help us to trust in Your power and to walk in faith, knowing that You are our healer and restorer. May Your healing and restoration bring glory to Your name and draw us closer to You each day.

In Jesus' name, we pray.

Amen.

CHAPTER 6
PRAYERS FOR PEACE AND COMFORT

God is the ultimate source of peace and comfort.

Introduction

In times of turmoil, uncertainty, and grief, the pursuit of peace and comfort becomes a deep and pressing need. The Bible offers profound assurance that God is the ultimate source of peace and comfort. Through prayer, we can access this divine peace and find solace in His presence. This chapter explores the biblical foundation for seeking peace and comfort, provides examples of such prayers, and offers practical steps to incorporate them into our daily lives.

The Biblical Foundation for Peace and Comfort

God as the Source of Peace

The Bible frequently describes God as the source of true peace. Jesus Himself said in John 14:27,

"Peace I leave with you; my peace I give to you. Not as the world gives do I give to you. Let not your hearts be troubled, neither let them be afraid."

This peace, unlike worldly peace, is deep, abiding, and transcends circumstances.

Comfort from God

God is also described as a comforter, particularly in times of trouble and sorrow. 2 Corinthians 1:3-4 proclaims,

"Blessed be the God and Father of our Lord Jesus Christ, the Father of mercies and God of all comfort, who comforts us in all our affliction."

This passage underscores God's role in providing comfort and His desire to soothe our hearts.

Prayers for Peace and Comfort

Prayers for Personal Peace

Praying for personal peace involves asking God to calm our anxieties and fill us with His tranquility.

Example: *"Heavenly Father, I come before You with a troubled heart. Please fill me with Your peace that*

surpasses all understanding. Calm my fears and anxieties, and help me to trust in Your unfailing love and faithfulness. May Your peace guard my heart and mind in Christ Jesus. Amen."

Prayers for Comfort in Grief

In times of loss and sorrow, praying for comfort invites God's soothing presence into our pain.

Example: *"Lord, I am hurting and grieving. I ask for Your comforting presence to surround me. Hold me close and give me the strength to endure this difficult time. Wipe away my tears and remind me of Your love and promise of eternal life. Bring peace to my heart and help me to find solace in You. Amen."*

Prayers for Peace in Troubled Times

When facing external turmoil or conflict, praying for peace invites God's intervention and reassurance.

Example: *"Father, I lift up the current situation to You, asking for Your peace to reign. In the midst of chaos and uncertainty, help me to find rest in You. Bring resolution to conflicts and calm to storms. Let Your peace prevail in my heart and in the world around me. I trust in Your sovereign power and Your plan for good.*

Amen."

Prayers for Comfort in Uncertainty

Uncertainty can be unsettling, but praying for comfort invites God's steadiness and hope.

Example: *"Lord, I feel uncertain and uneasy about the future. Please bring comfort to my heart and mind. Help me to trust in Your perfect plan and timing. Fill me with Your hope and assurance, knowing that You are in control. May Your comforting presence guide me through this season of uncertainty. Amen."*

Biblical Examples of Seeking Peace and Comfort

Jesus Calms the Storm

In Mark 4:35-41, Jesus calms a violent storm, bringing peace to His terrified disciples. This story illustrates Jesus' power to bring peace in the midst of chaos and His care for those who are afraid.

David's Psalms of Comfort

King David often sought God's comfort in times of distress. Psalm 23, one of the most beloved passages, declares,

"The Lord is my shepherd; I shall not want. He makes me lie down in green pastures. He leads me beside still waters. He restores my soul."

This psalm highlights God's role as a comforter and provider of peace.

Paul's Assurance of Peace

The Apostle Paul, despite facing numerous trials, often wrote about the peace of God. In Philippians 4:6-7, he encourages believers to present their requests to God with thanksgiving, promising that "the peace of God, which surpasses all understanding, will guard your hearts and your minds in Christ Jesus." Paul's example shows how prayer can bring peace even in challenging circumstances.

Practical Steps to Incorporate Prayers for Peace and Comfort

Establish a Prayer Routine

Creating a regular prayer routine helps us consistently seek God's peace and comfort. Set aside specific times each day to pray, focusing on inviting God's tranquility into your life.

Meditate on Scripture

Meditating on passages that speak of God's peace and comfort can bolster our prayers. Verses like Isaiah 26:3,

"You keep him in perfect peace whose mind is stayed on you, because he trusts in you,"

and 2 Corinthians 1:3-4,

Blessed be the God and Father of our Lord Jesus Christ, the Father of mercies and God of all comfort, who comforts us in all our tribulation, that we may be able to comfort those who are in any [a]trouble, with the comfort with which we ourselves are comforted by God.

can serve as anchors for our faith and reminders of God's promises.

Use Breathing Prayers

Breathing prayers combine deep, calming breaths with simple prayers for peace and comfort. For example, as you inhale, pray, "Lord, fill me with Your peace," and as you exhale, pray, "I release my worries to You." This practice can help reduce anxiety and invite God's presence.

Join a Prayer Group

Praying with others can provide additional support and encouragement. Join a prayer group where you can share your burdens and pray for peace and comfort together. The community aspect of group prayer can enhance the sense of God's presence and support.

Keep a Prayer Journal

Documenting your prayers for peace and comfort in a journal can help you track God's faithfulness and growth over time. Write down your prayers, any scriptures that comfort you, and how God responds. This practice can provide a tangible reminder of God's peace and comfort in your life.

Conclusion

Prayers for peace and comfort are vital in navigating life's challenges and uncertainties. The Bible assures us that God is our ultimate source of peace and comfort, and through prayer, we can access His calming presence. By incorporating these prayers into our daily lives, we invite God's peace to guard our hearts and minds, and His comfort to soothe our sorrows. May we continually seek His peace and comfort, trusting in His unfailing love and faithfulness.

Prayer

Heavenly Father,

We thank You for being our source of peace and comfort. In times of trouble and uncertainty, we seek Your calming presence. Fill our hearts with Your peace that surpasses all understanding and comfort us in our sorrows. Help us to trust in Your perfect plan and to find rest in Your loving arms. May Your peace and comfort guard our hearts and minds, drawing us closer to You each day.

In Jesus' name, we pray.

Amen.

PART III
PRAYERS FOR RELATIONSHIPS

CHAPTER 7
PRAYERS FOR FAMILY

Prayer is a powerful tool that can strengthen family bonds.

Introduction

Family is a foundational aspect of our lives, providing love, support, and a sense of belonging. However, families can also face challenges, conflicts, and trials. Prayer is a powerful tool that can strengthen family bonds, bring healing to broken relationships, and invite God's presence into our homes. This chapter explores the importance of praying for family, offers examples of prayers for various family needs, and provides practical steps to incorporate family prayer into daily life.

The Importance of Praying for Family

God's Design for Family

The Bible emphasizes the importance of family and God's design for it. Genesis 2:24 states,

"Therefore a man shall leave his father and his mother and hold fast to his wife, and they shall become one flesh."

The family unit is designed to reflect God's love and unity.

Strengthening Family Bonds

Prayer strengthens the bonds within a family by fostering communication, understanding, and love. Ephesians 4:2-3 encourages,

"Be completely humble and gentle; be patient, bearing with one another in love. Make every effort to keep the unity of the Spirit through the bond of peace."

Through prayer, families can seek God's guidance and strength to maintain unity and love.

Healing and Restoration

Families can face various challenges, from conflicts to health issues. Prayer invites God's healing and restorative power into these situations. James 5:16 reminds us,

"Therefore confess your sins to each other and pray for each other so that you may be healed. The prayer of a righteous person is powerful and effective."

Prayers for Family

Prayers for Family Unity

Seeking God's help in maintaining unity and love within the family is crucial.

Example: *"Heavenly Father, we ask for Your blessing on our family. Help us to love one another deeply and to remain united in Your love. Give us patience, understanding, and forgiveness in our interactions. May Your peace and unity dwell in our home, and may we reflect Your love to one another and the world. Amen."*

Prayers for Healing in the Family

Praying for healing, whether physical, emotional, or relational, invites God's restorative power into our families.

Example: *"Lord, we lift up our family to You, asking for Your healing touch. Heal any physical ailments, mend our broken relationships, and restore our emotional well-being. Help us to forgive one another and to seek reconciliation where there has been hurt. May Your healing power transform our family and bring us closer together. Amen."*

Prayers for Guidance and Protection

Asking for God's guidance and protection helps families navigate life's challenges and uncertainties.

Example: *"Father, we seek Your guidance and protection over our family. Lead us in Your ways and help us to make wise decisions. Protect us from harm and keep us safe in Your care. Give us the wisdom to follow Your path and the courage to trust in Your plan. Surround us with Your love and shield us from any danger. Amen."*

Prayers for Strength and Support

During difficult times, praying for strength and support can provide families with the resilience they need.

Example: *"Lord, we ask for Your strength and support as we face challenges in our family. Help us to lean on You and on each other for support. Give us the endurance to overcome obstacles and the faith to trust in Your provision. May Your strength sustain us, and may Your love encourage us through every trial. Amen."*

Biblical Examples of Family Prayer

Hannah's Prayer for a Child

Hannah's heartfelt prayer for a child in 1 Samuel 1:10-20 demonstrates the power of persistent prayer. God answered her plea, and she dedicated her son Samuel to the Lord. This story highlights the importance of bringing our deepest family desires to God in prayer.

Cornelius' Household Prayer

In Acts 10, Cornelius, a devout centurion, gathered his family and friends to hear Peter speak. As they prayed and listened, the Holy Spirit descended upon them, leading to their salvation. This example shows the impact of collective family prayer and the blessings that follow.

The Philippian Jailer's Family

In Acts 16:25-34, the Philippian jailer and his household were saved after Paul and Silas prayed and worshiped God. This event underscores the transformative power of prayer and the ripple effect it can have on an entire family.

Practical Steps to Incorporate Family Prayer

Establish a Family Prayer Routine

Creating a regular family prayer routine fosters a habit of seeking God together. Choose a time each day, such as before meals or bedtime, to gather and pray as a family.

Involve Everyone

Encourage all family members, including children, to participate in prayer. Allow each person to share his or her prayer requests and lead in prayer. This inclusion builds a sense of unity and shared spiritual growth.

Pray for Specific Needs

Focus on specific family needs during prayer. Whether it's a health issue, a relational conflict, or a significant decision, bringing these needs before God shows trust in His provision and care.

Use Scripture in Prayer

Incorporate scripture into family prayers to reinforce God's promises and guidance. Verses like Philippians 4:6-7,

"Do not be anxious about anything, but in every situation, by prayer and petition, with thanksgiving, present your requests to God,"

can provide a foundation for prayer.

Keep a Family Prayer Journal

Documenting family prayers and God's answers in a journal can be a powerful reminder of His faithfulness. Record prayer requests, answers, and any significant moments of spiritual growth.

Conclusion

Praying for family is essential in fostering unity, healing, guidance, and strength. The Bible offers numerous examples and encouragement to bring our family needs before God in prayer. By incorporating regular family prayer, involving all members, and focusing on specific needs, we invite God's presence and power into our homes. May we continually seek His blessings, trusting in His love and faithfulness to guide and sustain our families.

Prayer

Heavenly Father,

We thank You for the gift of family and for Your love that binds us together. As we seek Your presence in our family, we ask for Your guidance, healing, and strength. Help us to love one another deeply, to support each other through challenges, and to trust in Your provision. May Your peace and unity dwell in our home, and may we reflect Your love to the world around us. We trust in Your faithfulness and commit our family to Your care.

In Jesus' name, we pray.

Amen.

CHAPTER 8
PRAYERS FOR MARRIAGE

Through prayer, couples can seek God's guidance.

Introduction

Marriage is a sacred covenant designed by God to reflect His love and commitment. It is a union that requires nurturing, understanding, and constant communication. Prayer is a powerful tool that can strengthen marriages, bring healing to strained relationships, and invite God's presence into the marital bond. This chapter explores the significance of praying for marriage, provides examples of prayers for various marital needs, and offers practical steps to incorporate prayer into married life.

The Significance of Praying for Marriage

God's Design for Marriage

The Bible emphasizes that marriage is a divine institution. Genesis 2:24 declares,

"Therefore a man shall leave his father and his mother and hold fast to his wife, and they shall become one flesh."

This verse highlights the unity and commitment that characterize a godly marriage.

Strengthening Marital Bonds

Prayer strengthens the marital bond by fostering spiritual intimacy and mutual understanding. Ephesians 5:25-28 encourages,

"Husbands, love your wives, just as Christ loved the church and gave himself up for her to make her holy, cleansing[a] her by the washing with water through the word, and to present her to himself as a radiant church, without stain or wrinkle or any other blemish, but holy and blameless. In this same way, husbands ought to love their wives as their own bodies. He who loves his wife loves himself."

Through prayer, couples can seek God's guidance to love and honour each other deeply.

Healing and Restoration

Marriages, like all relationships, can face challenges and conflicts. Prayer invites God's healing and restorative power into these situations. Colossians 3:13 advises,

"Bear with each other and forgive one another if any of you has a grievance against someone. Forgive as the Lord forgave you."

Praying together fosters forgiveness and reconciliation.

Prayers for Marriage

Prayers for Unity and Love

Seeking God's help in maintaining unity and love within marriage is crucial.

Example: *"Heavenly Father, we thank You for the gift of our marriage. Help us to love each other deeply and to remain united in Your love. Give us patience, understanding, and forgiveness in our interactions. May Your peace and unity dwell in our relationship, and may we reflect Your love to one another and the world. Amen."*

Prayers for Healing and Forgiveness

Praying for healing and forgiveness invites God's grace into the marriage.

Example: *"Lord, we lift up our marriage to You, asking for Your healing touch. Heal any wounds caused by misunderstandings or hurtful words. Help us to forgive each other as You have forgiven us. Restore our relationship and draw us closer to each other and to You. Amen."*

Prayers for Guidance and Wisdom

Asking for God's guidance and wisdom helps couples navigate life's challenges.

Example: *"Father, we seek Your guidance and wisdom in our marriage. Lead us in Your ways and help us to make decisions that honour You. Give us the wisdom to handle conflicts with grace and the courage to trust in Your plan. Surround us with Your love and shield us from any harm. Amen."*

Prayers for Strength and Endurance

During difficult times, praying for strength and endurance can provide couples with the resilience they need.

Example: *"Lord, we ask for Your strength and endurance as we face challenges in our marriage. Help us to lean on You and on each other for support. Give us the perseverance to overcome obstacles and the faith to trust in Your provision. May Your strength sustain us, and may Your love encourage us through every trial. Amen."*

Biblical Examples of Praying for Marriage

Abraham and Sarah's Faith

Abraham and Sarah faced numerous challenges, including infertility and waiting on God's promises. Their faith and reliance on God's guidance (Genesis 15:1-6, 18:10-14) serve as a powerful example of a couple seeking God's direction and trusting in His timing.

After this, the word of the LORD came to Abram in a vision:

"Do not be afraid, Abram.
 I am your shield,
  your very great reward.

But Abram said, "Sovereign LORD, what can you give me since I remain childless and the one who will inherit[c] my estate is Eliezer of Damascus?" 3 And Abram said, "You have given me no children; so a servant in my household will be my heir."

Then the word of the LORD came to him: "This man will not be your heir, but a son who is your own flesh and blood will be your heir." He took him outside and said, "Look up at the sky and count the stars—if indeed you can count them." Then he said to him, "So shall your offspring be."

Abram believed the LORD, and he credited it to him as righteousness. **(Genesis 15:1-6, NIV)**.

Then one of them said, "I will surely return to you about this time next year, and Sarah your wife will have a son."

Now Sarah was listening at the entrance to the tent, which was behind him. Abraham and Sarah were already very old, and Sarah was past the age of childbearing. So Sarah laughed to herself as she thought, "After I am worn out and my lord is old, will I now have this pleasure?"

Then the LORD said to Abraham, "Why did Sarah laugh and say, 'Will I really have a child, now that I am old?' Is anything too hard for the LORD? I will return to you at the appointed time next year, and Sarah will have a son." **(Genesis 18:10-14, NIV)**.

Priscilla and Aquila's Partnership

Priscilla and Aquila, a married couple mentioned in Acts 18:2-3, worked together in ministry and supported each other in their faith journey. Their partnership and dedication to God's work highlight the importance of mutual support and shared spiritual goals in marriage.

Hannah and Elkanah's Devotion

Hannah and Elkanah's story in 1 Samuel 1:1-20 shows a couple united in prayer and devotion. Despite Hannah's initial barrenness, they sought God together, and their prayers were eventually answered with the birth of Samuel. This story emphasizes the power of persistent, united prayer in marriage.

Practical Steps to Incorporate Prayer in Marriage

Establish a Regular Prayer Routine

Creating a regular prayer routine fosters a habit of seeking God together. Choose a time each day, such as before meals or bedtime, to pray as a couple. This routine can strengthen your spiritual bond and keep God at the center of your relationship.

Pray for Each Other

Take time to pray specifically for each other's needs, dreams, and struggles. This practice can deepen your understanding and empathy for each other, fostering a stronger emotional connection.

Use Scripture in Prayer

Incorporate scripture into your prayers to reinforce God's promises and guidance. Verses like 1 Corinthians 13:4-7, which describe love's characteristics, can serve as a foundation for your prayers for marital love and unity.

Attend Prayer and Worship Together

Participating in church services, prayer meetings, and worship sessions together can enhance your spiritual intimacy and provide a shared faith experience. This practice can strengthen your bond and encourage spiritual growth.

Keep a Marriage Prayer Journal

Documenting your prayers for each other and your marriage in a journal can provide a tangible reminder of God's faithfulness. Record prayer requests, answers, and any significant moments of spiritual growth.

Conclusion

Praying for marriage is essential in fostering unity, healing, guidance, and strength. The Bible offers numerous examples and encouragement to bring our marital needs before God in prayer. By incorporating regular prayer routines, praying for each other, and focusing on specific needs, couples can invite God's presence and power into their relationship. May we continually seek His blessings, trusting in His love and faithfulness to guide and sustain our marriages.

Prayer

Heavenly Father,

We thank You for the gift of our marriage and for Your love that binds us together. As we seek Your presence in our relationship, we ask for Your guidance, healing, and strength. Help us to love each other deeply, to support each other through challenges, and to trust in Your provision. May Your peace and unity dwell in our marriage, and may we reflect Your love to the world around us. We trust in Your faithfulness and commit our marriage to Your care.

In Jesus' name, we pray.

Amen.

CHAPTER 9
PRAYERS FOR FRIENDSHIPS

Friendship offers joy, support, and a sense of belonging.

Introduction

Friendship is one of life's greatest gifts. It offers joy, support, and a sense of belonging. Friends celebrate our successes and provide comfort in times of trouble. This chapter includes prayers to nurture and deepen these precious relationships, seeking God's blessing and guidance in every aspect of our friendships.

Prayer for Gratitude in Friendship

Example Scenario: Emily is feeling especially grateful for her best friend, Sarah, who has been a constant source of support throughout her life. Sarah recently helped Emily through a difficult breakup, providing a listening ear and endless encouragement.

Prayer:

Heavenly Father,

Thank You for the blessing of friendships in my life. I am grateful for Sarah, whose kindness and support have been a source of strength and joy. May I always appreciate the love and care she offers. Help me to be a good friend in return, showing empathy, understanding, and love. May our friendship grow stronger each day, rooted in Your love and grace. Amen.

Prayer for Strengthening Bonds

Example Scenario: Michael and his college friends have drifted apart after graduation. He misses the closeness they once shared and hopes to rekindle those bonds.

Prayer:

Dear Lord,

I pray for my friendships, especially those that have grown distant. Help us to rebuild our connections on trust, honesty, and mutual respect. May we support one another through life's ups and downs. Guide us to communicate openly and resolve conflicts with love and understanding. Strengthen our bonds so that we may grow together in faith and love, reflecting Your light in the world. Amen.

Prayer for New Friendships

Example Scenario: Samantha has moved to a new city for work and feels lonely. She hopes to meet new people and build meaningful friendships.

Prayer:

Loving God,

As I start this new chapter in my life, I seek new friendships that will enrich my spirit and bring joy to my days. Lead me to people who share my values and passions, and with whom I can build meaningful connections. Help me to be open-hearted and welcoming, embracing new friends with kindness and grace. May our new friendships be a source of mutual growth, support, and joy. Amen.

Prayer for Healing and Reconciliation

Example Scenario: Alex and his childhood friend, Jordan, had a falling out over a misunderstanding. Alex misses their friendship and seeks reconciliation.

Prayer:

Merciful Father,

I lift up to You my friendship with Jordan, which has been strained by misunderstanding. Grant us the courage to seek forgiveness and the humility to extend it. Heal the wounds that have caused division and restore our relationship with Your love. Help us to rebuild trust and find new ways to connect. May our friendship be renewed and strengthened through Your grace. Amen.

Prayer for a Friend in Need

Example Scenario: Rachel's friend, Lisa, is going through a tough time at work and feels overwhelmed. Rachel wants to support Lisa through prayer.

Prayer:

Compassionate God,

I pray for my friend Lisa, who is going through a difficult time at work. Please provide her with comfort, strength, and hope. Surround her with Your love and peace, and guide her through her struggles. Help me to be a source of support and encouragement, offering a listening ear and a compassionate heart. May Lisa feel Your presence and know she is not alone. Amen.

Prayer for Long-Distance Friendships

Example Scenario: John and his childhood friend, Mike, live in different countries but maintain their close bond through regular calls and visits. John wants to strengthen their long-distance friendship.

Prayer:

Heavenly Father,

Distance may separate us, but my friendship with Mike remains strong. Thank You for the gift of long-distance friendships that withstand time and space. Help us to stay connected, communicate openly, and support each other despite the miles between us. May our friendship continue to grow and flourish, sustained by Your love and grace. Amen.

Prayer for Friendship with Christ

Example Scenario: Lily feels a strong connection to Jesus and wants to deepen her relationship with Him, viewing Him as her ultimate friend.

Prayer:

Lord Jesus,

You are the ultimate friend, always present and loving. Help me to build a deep and personal friendship with You. May I seek Your guidance in all things and trust in Your unfailing love. Teach me to be a true friend to others, reflecting Your compassion and kindness. In my friendships, may Your light shine through, bringing hope and love to all. Amen.

Conclusion

Friendships are a reflection of God's love and a vital part of our journey. Through these prayers, may we cherish, nurture, and strengthen the friendships that enrich our lives. Let us always be grateful for the friends we have and seek to be a source of love and support in their lives, just as Christ is to us.

Prayer

Gracious God,

Thank You for the gift of friendship, which enriches our lives in so many ways. As we pray for our friends, help us to be mindful of the love and support they provide. Grant us the wisdom and strength to be true and faithful friends in return. May our friendships be a source of joy, comfort, and growth, reflecting Your love in the world. Bless all our relationships, and help us to build connections that honour You and bring us closer to one another. In Your holy name, we pray.

Amen.

CHAPTER 10
PRAYERS FOR COMMUNITY

Through prayer, our communities can thrive in love, justice, and harmony.

Introduction

Community is the fabric that binds individuals together, creating a network of support, belonging, and shared purpose. It provides a sense of identity and fosters collaboration for the greater good. This chapter offers prayers for various aspects of community life, from celebrating unity and diversity to seeking strength and guidance in times of challenge. Through these prayers, we ask for God's blessing on our communities, that they may thrive in love, justice, and harmony.

Prayer for Unity in the Community

Example Scenario: The residents of a small town are coming together to address issues of local development. Despite differing opinions, they seek common ground and unity in their efforts.

Prayer:

Heavenly Father,

Thank You for the diverse community we are a part of. We pray for unity among us, that despite our differences, we may work together for the common good. Help us to listen with open hearts and to respect each other's perspectives. May we find strength in our diversity and build a community rooted in love, respect, and mutual support. Guide us to create a harmonious and thriving environment for all. Amen.

Prayer for Strength and Resilience

Example Scenario: A community has been hit by a natural disaster, and the residents are coming together to rebuild and support one another through the recovery process.

Prayer:

Dear Lord,

In times of trial and adversity, we turn to You for strength and resilience. Our community has faced significant challenges, and we ask for Your guidance as we rebuild and recover. Grant us the courage to support one another and the perseverance to overcome obstacles. May we emerge from this crisis stronger and more united, with a renewed sense of hope and purpose. Amen.

Prayer for Community Leaders

Example Scenario: Local leaders are preparing for an important meeting to discuss policies that will impact the entire community. They seek wisdom and guidance in their decision-making.

Prayer:

Loving God,

We lift up our community leaders to You, asking for Your wisdom and guidance as they make decisions that affect us all. Grant them the discernment to act justly and the courage to lead with integrity. Help them to listen to the voices of the community and to serve with compassion and fairness. May their efforts bring about positive change and prosperity for everyone. Amen.

Prayer for Peace and Harmony

Example Scenario: A neighbourhood has experienced tension and conflict due to cultural misunderstandings. Residents are seeking ways to foster peace and harmony.

Prayer:

Merciful Father,

We pray for peace and harmony in our community. Where there is division, bring understanding; where there is conflict, bring resolution. Help us to see each other through Your eyes, with love and compassion. May we work together to create a peaceful environment where everyone feels safe, respected, and valued. Guide us in our efforts to build bridges and to nurture a spirit of unity. Amen.

Prayer for Service and Volunteerism

Example Scenario: A community center is organizing a volunteer event to help those in need. Volunteers gather to serve and make a positive impact in their community.

Prayer:

Compassionate God,

We thank You for the spirit of service that inspires us to help those in need. Bless the volunteers in our community who give their time and talents to make a difference. May their efforts be fruitful and their hearts be filled with joy. Help us to recognize and address the needs around us, and to work together to create a community of care and support. In serving others, may we reflect Your love and grace. Amen.

Prayer for Celebrating Diversity

Example Scenario: A town is hosting its annual multicultural festival, celebrating the rich diversity of its residents and their unique cultural contributions.

Prayer:

Heavenly Father,

We celebrate the beautiful diversity within our community. Thank You for the unique cultures, traditions, and perspectives that enrich our lives. Help us to embrace our differences and to learn from one another. May our community be a place of inclusion, where everyone feels valued and respected. Guide us to celebrate our diversity in ways that foster understanding, unity, and love. Amen.

Prayer for Healing and Reconciliation

Example Scenario: Following a period of social unrest, community members are coming together for a healing and reconciliation event, seeking to address past hurts and build a more inclusive future.

Prayer:

Gracious God,

We come before You seeking healing and reconciliation for our community. Where there has been hurt, bring Your healing touch; where there has been division, bring Your peace. Help us to acknowledge past wrongs and to seek forgiveness and understanding. May we work towards a future where justice and compassion prevail. Bind us together in love and help us to create a community that reflects Your grace and mercy. Amen.

Conclusion

Community is the cornerstone of our social lives, providing support, identity, and purpose. Through these prayers, may we seek to strengthen and nurture the bonds that hold us together. Let us strive to create communities where love, justice, and harmony prevail, always guided by God's wisdom and grace.

Prayer

Almighty God,

We thank You for the gift of community and the sense of belonging it provides. As we lift up our communities in prayer, we ask for Your continued blessings and guidance. Help us to be active participants in building and nurturing our communities, always striving for unity, peace, and justice. May our efforts bring about positive change and reflect Your love in all we do. In Your holy name, we pray.

Amen.

PRAYERS FOR OUR TIME

PART IV
PRAYERS FOR
SPECIFIC NEEDS

CHAPTER 11
PRAYERS FOR TIMES OF CRISIS

Prayer can help us to cope in times of crisis.

Introduction

In times of crisis, our faith can provide solace and strength. Whether facing personal challenges, natural disasters, or societal upheavals, prayer helps us connect with God's presence, find hope, and seek guidance. This chapter offers prayers for various crises, aiming to bring comfort, courage, and clarity. Through these prayers, we invite God's healing and wisdom into our lives, trusting in His unwavering support during our darkest hours.

Prayer for Personal Crisis

Example Scenario: Jessica has recently lost her job and is feeling overwhelmed by the uncertainty of her future. She turns to prayer for comfort and direction.

Prayer:

Heavenly Father,

In this time of personal crisis, I feel lost and uncertain. Please grant me Your comfort and guidance. Help me to trust in Your plan and to find strength in Your presence. Give me the courage to face each day with hope and resilience. May I find new opportunities and paths that lead to a brighter future. Surround me with Your love and support, and help me to lean on You in this time of need. Amen.

Prayer for Natural Disasters

Example Scenario: A community has been devastated by a hurricane, and residents are coming together to support each other and begin the recovery process.

Prayer:

Dear Lord,

We come to You in the aftermath of this natural disaster, seeking Your comfort and strength. Please protect those affected and provide them with the resources they need to rebuild their lives. Give us the courage to support one another and the resilience to overcome this tragedy. May we find hope in Your presence and trust in Your unfailing love. Guide us in our efforts to heal and rebuild, and help us to emerge stronger and more united. Amen.

Prayer for Health Crises

Example Scenario: David's father has been diagnosed with a serious illness, and the family is struggling to cope with the news.

Prayer:

Compassionate God,

We lift up our prayers for David's father and all those facing health crises. Please grant them healing, comfort, and strength. Surround their families with Your love and support, and give them the courage to face each day with hope. Guide the hands of doctors and caregivers, and provide wisdom and clarity in their decisions. May Your peace fill our hearts, and may we trust in Your healing power. Amen.

Prayer for Societal Unrest

Example Scenario: The nation is experiencing significant social unrest, and communities are divided and in turmoil.

Prayer:

Loving God,

In these times of societal unrest, we seek Your peace and justice. Help us to listen to one another with open hearts and to work towards understanding and reconciliation. Grant our leaders wisdom and courage to act with integrity and fairness. May Your love guide us in our actions and words, and may we strive for a society where justice and compassion prevail. Bring healing to our divided communities and help us to build a future rooted in Your love. Amen.

Prayer for Financial Crisis

Example Scenario: Mark and his family are struggling with severe financial difficulties and are unsure how they will make ends meet.

Prayer:

Gracious God,

We turn to You in this time of financial crisis, seeking Your provision and guidance. Please help Mark and his family to find the resources they need and to trust in Your plan. Grant them wisdom in their decisions and the strength to persevere through these challenges. May they find comfort in Your presence and hope in Your promises. Surround them with supportive community and opportunities for a brighter future. Amen.

Prayer for Mental Health Crisis

Example Scenario: Emma is experiencing severe anxiety and depression, feeling overwhelmed and isolated.

Prayer:

Merciful Father,

We lift up Emma and all those facing mental health crises. Please bring them Your healing and peace. Surround them with supportive people who can offer love and understanding. Give them the strength to seek help and the courage to face each day. May Your presence bring comfort and hope, and may they find solace in Your unfailing love. Guide us all to be compassionate and supportive to those in need. Amen.

Prayer for Global Crises

Example Scenario: A global pandemic has caused widespread fear and uncertainty, impacting lives around the world.

Prayer:

Almighty God,

In the face of this global crisis, we seek Your wisdom and strength. Please protect those who are vulnerable and provide for those in need. Grant wisdom to our leaders and health professionals as they navigate these challenging times. Help us to act with compassion and solidarity, supporting one another through these difficulties. May Your peace fill our hearts, and may we trust in Your guidance and care. Bring healing to our world and restore hope in our hearts. Amen.

Conclusion

Crisis can strike unexpectedly, leaving us feeling vulnerable and uncertain. Through these prayers, we seek God's presence, guidance, and strength. May we find comfort in His love and resilience in our faith, trusting that He will carry us through our darkest hours.

Prayer

Heavenly Father,

We thank You for being our refuge and strength in times of crisis. As we lift up our prayers, we ask for Your continued presence and guidance. Help us to trust in Your unfailing love and to find hope in Your promises. May we support one another with compassion and courage, always seeking Your wisdom and peace. In Your holy name, we pray.

Amen.

CHAPTER 12
PRAYERS FOR THE WORKPLACE

Through prayer, we can invite God's presence into our work lives.

Introduction

Work is an integral part of our lives, shaping our daily routines and providing a sense of purpose and achievement. It also presents its own set of challenges and opportunities for growth. This chapter offers prayers for various aspects of the workplace, from seeking guidance in our tasks to fostering harmonious relationships with colleagues. Through these prayers, we invite God's presence into our professional lives, seeking His wisdom, strength, and blessings in all we do.

Prayer for Guidance in Work

Example Scenario: Anna is starting a new project at work and feels overwhelmed by the complexity and expectations. She seeks God's guidance to navigate her responsibilities successfully.

Prayer:

Heavenly Father,

As I embark on this new project, I seek Your guidance and wisdom. Help me to understand my tasks and to approach my work with clarity and focus. Grant me the ability to manage my time effectively and to find solutions to the challenges I may face. May Your presence be with me, providing strength and insight. Help me to do my best and to honor You in all I do. Amen.

Prayer for Workplace Relationships

Example Scenario: James is experiencing tension with a coworker, and it is affecting the overall atmosphere in the office. He prays for peace and understanding.

Prayer:

Dear Lord,

I lift up my workplace relationships to You, especially where there is tension and misunderstanding. Help me to approach my colleagues with patience, kindness, and respect. Grant us the ability to communicate openly and to resolve conflicts with grace. May our interactions be guided by Your love, fostering a harmonious and supportive work environment. Help us to work together effectively and to build positive relationships. Amen.

Prayer for Strength and Endurance

Example Scenario: Maria is facing a particularly busy and stressful period at work, with numerous deadlines and high expectations.

Prayer:

Loving God,

In this busy and stressful time, I seek Your strength and endurance. Help me to manage my responsibilities with grace and to stay focused amidst the pressure. Grant me the energy to meet my deadlines and the resilience to overcome any challenges. May I find moments of peace in Your presence, and may Your strength sustain me through this demanding period. Amen.

Prayer for Integrity and Excellence

Example Scenario: Thomas works in a competitive industry where he faces ethical dilemmas and the temptation to cut corners to get ahead.

Prayer:

Gracious God,

Help me to maintain integrity and excellence in my work. Grant me the courage to make ethical decisions and to uphold my values, even when it is difficult. May I strive for excellence in all I do, reflecting Your standards of honesty and diligence. Help me to be a positive example to my colleagues and to contribute to a workplace culture of integrity and respect. Amen.

Prayer for Finding Purpose in Work

Example Scenario: Linda feels unfulfilled in her current job and is struggling to find a sense of purpose and meaning in her daily tasks.

Prayer:

Heavenly Father,

I seek Your guidance in finding purpose and meaning in my work. Help me to see the value in my tasks and to understand how my efforts contribute to the greater good. May I find joy and fulfillment in my daily responsibilities, knowing that I am serving You through my work. Guide me to opportunities where I can use my gifts and talents to make a positive impact. Amen.

Prayer for Workplace Safety

Example Scenario: John works in a construction site where safety is a constant concern. He prays for protection for himself and his coworkers.

Prayer:

Dear Lord,

I pray for safety in my workplace, especially for those in hazardous environments. Protect us from accidents and injuries, and grant us the wisdom to follow safety protocols diligently. Help us to look out for one another and to create a safe and secure work environment. May Your protection be with us each day, and may we trust in Your care. Amen.

Prayer for Career Growth and Opportunities

Example Scenario: Rachel is considering a career change and is looking for new opportunities that align with her skills and passions.

Prayer:

Loving God,

I seek Your guidance in my career growth and opportunities. Help me to discern the right path and to recognize the opportunities that align with my skills and passions. Grant me the courage to take steps towards new challenges and the wisdom to make informed decisions. May my career journey be guided by Your hand, leading me to fulfillment and success. Amen.

Conclusion

The workplace is a significant part of our lives, filled with both challenges and opportunities. Through these prayers, we invite God's presence into our professional lives, seeking His wisdom, strength, and blessings. May we strive to honor Him in all we do, fostering positive relationships, maintaining integrity, and finding purpose in our work.

Prayer

Almighty God,

We thank You for the gift of work and the opportunities it provides for growth and service. As we lift up our workplace prayers, we ask for Your continued guidance and blessings. Help us to honor You in our professional lives, striving for excellence, integrity, and harmony. May we support one another and create positive environments where everyone can thrive. In Your holy name, we pray.

Amen.

CHAPTER 13
PRAYERS FOR FINANCIAL STABILITY

Invite God's wisdom and blessings into your financial lives.

Introduction

Financial stability is a cornerstone of a secure and peaceful life. It allows us to meet our needs, plan for the future, and support those we care about. Yet, financial challenges can bring stress and uncertainty. This chapter offers prayers for various aspects of financial stability, from seeking God's guidance in managing our resources to finding peace and trust in His provision. Through these prayers, we invite God's wisdom and blessings into our financial lives.

Prayer for Financial Wisdom

Example Scenario: Sophia is learning to manage her finances better and seeks God's guidance to make wise decisions.

Prayer:

Heavenly Father,

I seek Your wisdom in managing my finances. Help me to make sound decisions that honor You and provide for my needs. Guide me to use my resources responsibly and to avoid unnecessary debt. Teach me to save and invest wisely, and to trust in Your provision. May I always remember that all I have is a gift from You, and use it to glorify Your name. Amen.

Prayer for Provision

Example Scenario: Mark has lost his job and is worried about how he will provide for his family. He turns to God for comfort and provision.

Prayer:

Dear Lord,

I come to You in my time of need, asking for Your provision and care. Please open doors for new employment opportunities and provide the resources my family needs. Help us to trust in Your faithfulness and to find peace in Your promises. May we experience Your abundant provision, and may it strengthen our faith in You. Guide us through this challenging time and help us to see Your hand at work in our lives. Amen.

Prayer for Financial Breakthrough

Example Scenario: Rachel has been struggling with mounting debts and is praying for a financial breakthrough to ease her burden.

Prayer:

Loving God,

I lift up my financial burdens to You, asking for a breakthrough. Please provide the means to pay off my debts and to restore my financial stability. Grant me opportunities for additional income and the discipline to manage my resources well. Help me to trust in Your timing and to remain faithful, knowing that You are my provider. May Your blessings overflow in my life, bringing relief and renewed hope. Amen.

Prayer for Contentment and Gratitude

Example Scenario: John often feels anxious about money, always wanting more even though he has enough to meet his needs. He seeks to cultivate contentment and gratitude.

Prayer:

Gracious God,

Help me to find contentment in what I have and to trust in Your provision. Teach me to be grateful for the blessings I receive each day and to focus on the abundance rather than the lack. May I learn to live simply and generously, sharing with others from a heart of gratitude. Help me to find joy in Your presence and to trust that You will always provide for my needs. Amen.

Prayer for Financial Discipline

Example Scenario: Emma struggles with impulsive spending and wants to develop better financial discipline.

Prayer:

Heavenly Father,

I seek Your help in developing financial discipline. Grant me the self-control to manage my spending and to prioritize my needs over my wants. Help me to create and stick to a budget, and to save diligently for the future. May I be a good steward of the resources You have entrusted to me, using them wisely and responsibly. Guide me in making choices that honor You and contribute to my financial well-being. Amen.

Prayer for Generosity

Example Scenario: Michael has been blessed with financial abundance and seeks to use his wealth to help others and support good causes.

Prayer:

Dear Lord,

Thank You for the financial blessings You have given me. Help me to use my resources generously to support those in need and to advance Your kingdom. Guide me in identifying opportunities to give and to make a positive impact. May my generosity reflect Your love and grace, and bring hope and joy to others. Teach me to hold my wealth with open hands, always ready to share and serve. Amen.

Prayer for Trust in God's Provision

Example Scenario: Linda is anxious about her financial future and wants to deepen her trust in God's provision.

Prayer:

Loving God,

In times of financial uncertainty, help me to trust in Your provision. Remind me that You are my provider and that You know my needs even before I ask. Help me to release my worries and to rest in Your promises. May I have faith that You will supply all my needs according to Your riches in glory. Guide me to make wise choices and to trust in Your faithfulness each day. Amen.

Conclusion

Financial stability is a vital aspect of our lives, impacting our well-being and peace of mind. Through these prayers, we seek God's wisdom, provision, and blessings in our financial endeavours. May we learn to trust in His faithful care, to manage our resources wisely, and to live with contentment and generosity.

Prayer

Almighty God,

We thank You for Your constant provision and care in our lives. As we lift up our financial prayers, we ask for Your guidance and blessings. Help us to trust in Your faithfulness and to manage our resources wisely. May we find contentment in Your provision and generosity in our hearts. Guide us in all our financial decisions, and may we honor You in all we do. In Your holy name, we pray.

Amen.

CHAPTER 14
PRAYERS FOR MENTAL HEALTH

Through prayers, we seek to nurture our mental health.

Introduction

Mental health is a crucial aspect of our overall well-being, impacting our thoughts, emotions, and behaviors. In times of stress, anxiety, or depression, turning to prayer can bring comfort, strength, and healing. This chapter offers prayers for various aspects of mental health, inviting God's peace, guidance, and love into our minds and hearts. Through these prayers, we seek to nurture our mental health and find solace in God's presence.

Prayer for Peace of Mind

Example Scenario: Sarah is overwhelmed with anxiety about her future, finding it difficult to quiet her racing thoughts.

Prayer:

Heavenly Father,

I come to You seeking peace of mind. My thoughts are racing, and I feel overwhelmed by anxiety. Please calm my mind and fill me with Your peace. Help me to trust in Your plan and to find rest in Your presence. Guide me to focus on Your promises and to release my worries to You. May Your peace, which surpasses all understanding, guard my heart and mind in Christ Jesus. Amen.

Prayer for Strength in Depression

Example Scenario: David is battling depression and struggles to find hope and motivation in his daily life.

Prayer:

Dear Lord,

In the depths of my depression, I seek Your strength and comfort. It is hard to find hope and motivation, and I feel weighed down by sadness. Please lift me out of this darkness and fill me with Your light. Give me the strength to face each day and the courage to seek help. Surround me with Your love and the support of others who care. May Your presence bring me healing and hope. Amen.

Prayer for Overcoming Fear

Example Scenario: Emily is paralyzed by fear and finds it difficult to engage in activities she once enjoyed.

Prayer:

Loving God,

Fear has taken hold of my heart, and I feel paralyzed by its grip. I ask for Your help in overcoming this fear. Fill me with Your courage and strength. Remind me that You are with me always, and that Your perfect love casts out fear. Help me to take small steps towards overcoming my anxieties and to trust in Your protection and guidance. May I find freedom and peace in Your love. Amen.

Prayer for Clarity and Focus

Example Scenario: Michael struggles with concentration and clarity, making it difficult to complete tasks at work and at home.

Prayer:

Heavenly Father,

I seek Your help in finding clarity and focus. My mind feels scattered, and I struggle to concentrate on my tasks. Please clear away the mental fog and help me to find focus. Guide me in organizing my thoughts and prioritizing my responsibilities. May Your wisdom and clarity fill my mind, enabling me to work effectively and purposefully. Amen.

Prayer for Emotional Healing

Example Scenario: Linda is carrying emotional wounds from past experiences and seeks healing and wholeness.

Prayer:

Compassionate God,

I come to You with a heart burdened by emotional wounds. The pain of past experiences weighs heavily on me. Please bring Your healing touch to my heart and mind. Help me to forgive those who have hurt me and to release any bitterness or anger. Fill me with Your love and peace, and restore my emotional well-being. May I find wholeness in Your presence and move forward with hope and joy. Amen.

Prayer for Managing Stress

Example Scenario: Mark is under a lot of stress at work and home, feeling overwhelmed by his responsibilities.

Prayer:

Gracious God,

The stress I am under feels overwhelming, and I struggle to manage my responsibilities. I ask for Your help in finding balance and peace. Grant me the wisdom to prioritize my tasks and the strength to handle them effectively. Help me to find moments of rest and renewal in Your presence. May Your peace fill my heart and mind, and may I trust in Your provision and care. Amen.

Prayer for Self-Acceptance

Example Scenario: Rachel struggles with self-esteem and acceptance, often feeling unworthy and inadequate.

Prayer:

Dear Lord,

I struggle with feelings of unworthiness and inadequacy. Help me to see myself through Your eyes, as Your beloved child. Grant me the grace to accept myself and to recognize my worth in You. Help me to let go of negative self-talk and to embrace the person You have created me to be. May Your love and acceptance fill my heart, giving me confidence and peace. Amen.

Prayer for Seeking Professional Help

Example Scenario: James is considering seeking therapy for his mental health struggles but feels unsure about taking that step.

Prayer:

Loving God,

I am considering seeking professional help for my mental health struggles, but I feel unsure and anxious about taking this step. Please guide me in this decision and give me the courage to seek the support I need. Help me to find a compassionate and skilled professional who can assist me on this journey. May Your wisdom and peace be with me as I take steps towards healing and wholeness. Amen.

Conclusion

Mental health is a vital aspect of our well-being, deserving of care and attention. Through these prayers, we invite God's healing, peace, and strength into our minds and hearts. May we find solace in His presence and the courage to seek help and support when needed. Trusting in God's love and guidance, we can nurture our mental health and live with hope and joy.

Prayer

Heavenly Father,

We thank You for Your constant presence and love in our lives. As we lift up our prayers for mental health, we ask for Your healing and peace. Help us to trust in Your guidance and to find strength in Your promises. May we nurture our mental well-being and support one another with compassion and care. In Your holy name, we pray.

Amen.

PART V
PRAYERS FOR SPIRITUAL LIFE

PRAYERS FOR OUR TIME

CHAPTER 15
PRAYERS FOR DAILY DEVOTION

Daily devotion helps to deepen our spiritual journey.

Introduction

Daily devotion is a practice that nurtures our relationship with God, providing spiritual nourishment and guidance. By setting aside time each day for prayer, reflection, and reading Scripture, we can draw closer to God and strengthen our faith. This chapter offers prayers for various aspects of daily devotion, helping to deepen our spiritual journey and keep our hearts aligned with God's will.

Morning Prayer for a New Day

Example Scenario: Emma starts her day with a prayer to invite God's presence and guidance throughout the day.

Prayer:

Heavenly Father,

Thank You for the gift of a new day. As I begin my day, I invite Your presence into every moment. Guide my thoughts, words, and actions, so that they may honor You. Grant me the wisdom to make good decisions and the strength to face any challenges. May I find joy in Your blessings and opportunities to share Your love with others. Fill my heart with gratitude and peace, knowing that You are with me always. Amen.

Prayer for Spiritual Growth

Example Scenario: James seeks to grow in his faith and deepen his understanding of God's word.

Prayer:

Dear Lord,

I desire to grow closer to You and deepen my understanding of Your word. Help me to be diligent in my daily devotions and to seek You with all my heart. Open my eyes to the truths in Scripture and teach me Your ways. May Your Holy Spirit guide me in my study and reflection, drawing me closer to You each day. Strengthen my faith and help me to live out Your teachings in my daily life. Amen.

Prayer for Patience and Peace

Example Scenario: Sophia often feels rushed and stressed throughout her day, seeking God's peace and patience.

Prayer:

Loving God,

In the busyness of life, I seek Your peace and patience. Help me to slow down and to find moments of quiet in Your presence. Fill my heart with Your peace that surpasses all understanding, and grant me the patience to handle each situation with grace. May I reflect Your love and kindness in my interactions with others. Teach me to trust in Your timing and to find rest in Your promises. Amen.

Prayer for Guidance and Wisdom

Example Scenario: Mark faces important decisions and seeks God's wisdom and guidance in making the right choices.

Prayer:

Gracious God,

I come to You seeking Your wisdom and guidance. I have important decisions to make, and I need Your direction. Help me to discern Your will and to choose the path that aligns with Your purpose for my life. Grant me clarity of mind and peace in my heart as I make these choices. May Your Holy Spirit guide me and give me the confidence to follow where You lead. Amen.

Prayer for Gratitude and Contentment

Example Scenario: Rachel wants to cultivate a heart of gratitude and contentment, focusing on her blessings rather than her worries.

Prayer:

Dear Lord,

Thank You for the many blessings You have given me. Help me to cultivate a heart of gratitude and to focus on the good things in my life. Teach me to be content with what I have and to trust in Your provision. May I always remember that true contentment comes from knowing and loving You. Fill my heart with joy and peace, and help me to share my blessings with others. Amen.

Prayer for Strength and Resilience

Example Scenario: Michael is facing a difficult period and needs strength and resilience to persevere.

Prayer:

Heavenly Father,

I am going through a challenging time and need Your strength and resilience. Help me to persevere and to trust in Your faithfulness. Grant me the courage to face each day and the determination to overcome these obstacles. May Your presence be my source of strength and comfort. Remind me that I can do all things through Christ who strengthens me. Amen.

Prayer for Evening Reflection

Example Scenario: Linda concludes her day with a prayer, reflecting on the day's events and seeking God's peace before sleep.

Prayer:

Loving God,

As I end this day, I take a moment to reflect on all that has happened. Thank You for Your presence and guidance throughout the day. I lift up to You any worries or concerns, asking for Your peace and comfort. Forgive me for any mistakes I made, and help me to learn from them. As I prepare for sleep, may Your peace fill my heart and mind. Grant me restful sleep and renew my spirit for the new day ahead. Amen.

Prayer for Devotional Consistency

Example Scenario: John struggles to maintain a consistent devotional practice and seeks God's help to stay committed.

Prayer:

Gracious God,

I desire to be consistent in my daily devotions, but I often struggle to maintain this practice. Help me to prioritize my time with You and to stay committed to my spiritual growth. Give me the discipline to set aside moments each day for prayer, reflection, and reading Scripture. May my relationship with You deepen as I consistently seek Your presence. Strengthen my resolve and fill my heart with a longing to know You more. Amen.

Conclusion

Daily devotion is a powerful way to nurture our relationship with God and grow in faith. Through these prayers, we seek to invite God's presence into our daily lives, finding strength, peace, and guidance. May our hearts be continually drawn to Him, and may we experience His love and grace in every moment.

Prayer

Heavenly Father,

We thank You for the opportunity to draw closer to You through daily devotion. As we lift up our prayers, we ask for Your guidance and blessings. Help us to stay committed to our spiritual practice and to seek You with all our hearts. May our daily devotions deepen our faith and fill us with Your peace, wisdom, and love. In Your holy name, we pray.

Amen.

CHAPTER 16
PRAYERS FOR WORSHIP AND PRAISE

Let us celebrate God's majesty, faithfulness, and everlasting love.

Introduction

Worship and praise are essential expressions of our love and reverence for God. They allow us to acknowledge His greatness, offer gratitude, and deepen our connection with Him. This chapter provides prayers for various aspects of worship and praise, encouraging us to lift our hearts in adoration and thanksgiving. Through these prayers, we celebrate God's majesty, faithfulness, and love, fostering a spirit of worship in our daily lives.

Prayer of Adoration

Example Scenario: Sarah begins her morning devotion by focusing on God's majesty and holiness.

Prayer:

Heavenly Father,

I come before You in awe of Your majesty and holiness. You are the Creator of the universe, and Your power and wisdom are beyond understanding. I adore You for who You are—eternal, unchanging, and full of grace. May my heart be continually filled with reverence and wonder at Your greatness. I lift up my voice in adoration, praising You with all that I am. Amen.

Prayer of Thanksgiving

Example Scenario: Mark reflects on the blessings in his life and expresses gratitude to God.

Prayer:

Loving God,

Thank You for the countless blessings You have poured into my life. I am grateful for Your provision, guidance, and unfailing love. Thank You for my family, friends, and the opportunities You have given me. Help me to always remember Your goodness and to express my gratitude in all circumstances. May my heart overflow with thanksgiving, and may my life be a testament to Your faithfulness. Amen.

Prayer of Praise in Difficult Times

Example Scenario: Rachel is going through a challenging period but chooses to praise God despite her circumstances.

Prayer:

Gracious God,

Even in the midst of difficulties, I choose to praise You. I know that You are with me, and Your love never fails. Help me to see Your hand at work in my life, even when times are tough. I praise You for Your faithfulness and Your promises that bring hope and comfort. Strengthen my faith and help me to trust in Your plan. May my praise be a beacon of light, shining Your love and grace to others. Amen.

Prayer for a Heart of Worship

Example Scenario: John desires to cultivate a heart that continually seeks to worship God in all aspects of life.

Prayer:

Heavenly Father,

I long to have a heart that continually seeks to worship You. Help me to see every moment as an opportunity to glorify You. Teach me to worship You not only in prayer and song but in my actions and choices. May my life be a reflection of Your love and grace, and may my heart be ever filled with praise for You. Guide me to live in a way that honors and exalts Your holy name. Amen.

Prayer for Corporate Worship

Example Scenario: Emily looks forward to attending church and joining her community in worship.

Prayer:

Dear Lord,

Thank You for the gift of community and the opportunity to gather with others to worship You. As I join my church family in praise, may our hearts be united in adoration and thanksgiving. Help us to encourage one another and to lift each other up in faith. May our worship be a pleasing offering to You, and may Your presence fill our gathering. Strengthen our bonds and deepen our love for You and each other. Amen.

Prayer for Worship Leaders

Example Scenario: Michael, a worship leader, seeks God's guidance and inspiration for leading the congregation in worship.

Prayer:

Gracious God,

Thank You for the privilege of leading others in worship. I seek Your guidance and inspiration as I prepare to lead our congregation. Fill me with Your Holy Spirit, and may my heart be in tune with Yours. Help me to choose songs and words that honour You and draw others closer to You. May Your presence be felt in our worship, and may lives be transformed by Your love. Guide me to lead with humility and joy, always pointing others to You. Amen.

Prayer for Praise in Creation

Example Scenario: Linda finds inspiration in nature and praises God for the beauty of His creation.

Prayer:

Loving Creator,

I am in awe of the beauty and wonder of Your creation. The majesty of the mountains, the serenity of the seas, and the intricacy of every living thing speak of Your greatness. Thank You for the gift of nature that reflects Your glory. Help me to see Your handiwork in all that surrounds me and to praise You for Your creativity and love. May my heart be filled with wonder and gratitude as I experience the world You have made. Amen.

Prayer for Continuous Praise

Example Scenario: James wants to cultivate an attitude of continuous praise throughout his day.

Prayer:

Heavenly Father,

I desire to live a life of continuous praise. Help me to recognize Your presence in every moment and to respond with gratitude and worship. May my thoughts, words, and actions be an offering of praise to You. Teach me to find joy in Your presence and to celebrate Your goodness in all circumstances. Let my life be a song of praise that brings glory to Your name. Amen.

Conclusion

Worship and praise are powerful expressions of our love for God and our acknowledgment of His greatness. Through these prayers, we seek to cultivate a heart of worship, offering adoration, thanksgiving, and praise to our Creator. May our lives be filled with continuous worship, and may we find joy and peace in His presence.

Prayer

Almighty God,

We thank You for the privilege of worshiping and praising You. As we lift up our prayers of worship and praise, we ask for Your presence and blessings. Help us to cultivate a heart of worship and to live lives that honor and glorify You. May our praise be a sweet offering to You, and may we draw closer to You each day. In Your holy name, we pray.

Amen.

CHAPTER 17
PRAYERS FOR CONFESSION AND REPENTANCE

Confession and repentance help us to humble ourselves before God.

Introduction

Confession and repentance are fundamental aspects of our spiritual journey. They allow us to acknowledge our sins, seek God's forgiveness, and turn our hearts back to Him. This chapter provides prayers for various aspects of confession and repentance, helping us to humble ourselves before God and receive His mercy and grace. Through these prayers, we find spiritual renewal and a closer relationship with our Heavenly Father.

Prayer of Confession

Example Scenario: Emma feels the weight of her sins and seeks God's forgiveness through heartfelt confession.

Prayer:

Merciful God,

I come before You with a heavy heart, acknowledging my sins and shortcomings. I confess that I have strayed from Your ways and have failed to live according to Your will. Forgive me for the times I have hurt others, neglected Your word, and acted out of selfishness. Cleanse me from my sins and renew a right spirit within me. Help me to walk in Your light and to seek Your righteousness in all I do. Amen.

Prayer for Genuine Repentance

Example Scenario: Mark realizes the need for genuine repentance and seeks God's help to turn away from his sinful habits.

Prayer:

Heavenly Father,

I recognize my need for genuine repentance. I have fallen into sinful habits that distance me from You. Help me to turn away from these behaviors and to seek Your righteousness. Grant me the strength and determination to change my ways and to live a life that honors You. Create in me a clean heart and renew a steadfast spirit within me. May Your grace lead me to true repentance and transformation. Amen.

Prayer for Forgiveness

Example Scenario: Rachel struggles with guilt and seeks God's forgiveness for her past mistakes.

Prayer:

Loving God,

I am burdened by guilt and regret for the mistakes I have made. I seek Your forgiveness and mercy. Help me to let go of my past and to embrace Your grace. Remind me that Your love is unconditional and that Your forgiveness is always available. Wash away my sins and restore my soul. May Your forgiveness bring healing and peace to my heart. Amen.

Prayer for Strength to Resist Temptation

Example Scenario: John faces frequent temptations and asks for God's strength to resist them.

Prayer:

Gracious God,

I face temptations that challenge my faith and integrity. I ask for Your strength to resist these temptations and to stay true to Your ways. Fill me with Your Holy Spirit, and guide me to make choices that honor You. Help me to remember Your promises and to find refuge in Your word. May Your presence be my source of strength and courage. Amen.

Prayer for a Humble Heart

Example Scenario: Emily seeks to cultivate humility and acknowledges her need for God's grace in her life.

Prayer:

Heavenly Father,

I come to You with a humble heart, acknowledging my need for Your grace. Help me to let go of pride and to embrace humility. Teach me to rely on Your strength and not on my own understanding. May I always seek to glorify You rather than myself. Fill my heart with gratitude and humility, recognizing that all I have is a gift from You. Amen.

Prayer for Reconciliation

Example Scenario: Michael seeks reconciliation with a friend after a misunderstanding and asks for God's guidance and forgiveness.

Prayer:

Dear Lord,

I seek reconciliation with [Name] after our misunderstanding. Help me to approach them with humility and a sincere heart. Grant us both the grace to forgive and to seek understanding. May Your love guide our conversation and bring healing to our relationship. Help us to rebuild trust and to move forward in harmony. Thank You for Your forgiveness and for teaching us to forgive others. Amen.

Prayer for Inner Healing

Example Scenario: Linda feels the deep wounds of past sins and seeks God's healing and restoration.

Prayer:

Compassionate God,

I carry deep wounds from past sins that weigh heavily on my heart. I seek Your healing and restoration. Touch my heart with Your love and grace, and heal the brokenness within me. Help me to forgive myself and to embrace Your forgiveness. May Your healing power renew my spirit and bring peace to my soul. Guide me towards wholeness and joy in Your presence. Amen.

Prayer for Daily Renewal

Example Scenario: James wants to make confession and repentance a daily practice in his spiritual life.

Prayer:

Heavenly Father,

I desire to make confession and repentance a daily practice in my life. Help me to examine my heart each day and to bring my sins before You. Grant me the humility to confess my wrongdoings and the strength to turn away from them. Fill me with Your Holy Spirit and guide me towards righteousness. May Your grace renew me each day, drawing me closer to You. Amen.

Conclusion

Confession and repentance are vital for spiritual growth and renewal. Through these prayers, we seek God's forgiveness, strength, and guidance, turning our hearts back to Him. May we embrace His grace and mercy, allowing His love to transform our lives and draw us closer to Him.

Prayer

Loving and Merciful God,

We thank You for the gift of confession and repentance. As we lift up our prayers, we ask for Your forgiveness and grace. Help us to humble ourselves before You and to seek Your righteousness. May Your love and mercy renew our hearts and draw us closer to You each day. In Your holy name, we pray.

Amen.

CHAPTER 18
PRAYERS FOR SPIRITUAL WARFARE

Through prayer, we can stand firm in our faith, resist the enemy, and claim victory.

Introduction

Spiritual warfare is a reality for every believer, involving the battles we face against the forces of darkness. Through prayer, we can stand firm in our faith, resist the enemy, and claim victory through the power of Jesus Christ. This chapter provides prayers for various aspects of spiritual warfare, equipping us to combat the challenges and temptations we encounter. With these prayers, we seek God's protection, strength, and guidance, confident in His promise to be our defender.

Prayer for Protection

Example Scenario: Emma feels spiritually vulnerable and seeks God's protection against any spiritual attacks.

Prayer:

Heavenly Father,

I seek Your divine protection against any spiritual attacks. Surround me with Your shield of faith and guard my heart and mind from the enemy's schemes. Cover me with Your armor and help me to stand firm in Your truth. Keep me safe from harm and guide me in Your righteousness. Thank You for being my refuge and my strength. Amen.

Prayer for Strength and Courage

Example Scenario: Mark is facing a difficult situation that requires spiritual strength and courage.

Prayer:

Dear Lord,

I am confronted with challenges that test my faith and resolve. I ask for Your strength and courage to face these trials. Fill me with Your Holy Spirit and empower me to stand firm. Remind me that I am not alone and that Your strength is made perfect in my weakness. Help me to be bold in my faith and to trust in Your mighty power. Amen.

Prayer to Resist Temptation

Example Scenario: Rachel is struggling with recurring temptations and seeks God's help to overcome them.

Prayer:

Gracious God,

I am battling temptations that seek to lead me astray. I ask for Your help to resist these urges and to stay true to Your ways. Strengthen my willpower and remind me of Your promises. Help me to turn away from sin and to seek Your righteousness. Equip me with the spiritual armor I need to withstand these attacks and to remain faithful to You. Amen.

Prayer for Discernment

Example Scenario: John needs discernment to recognize the subtle deceptions of the enemy in his daily life.

Prayer:

Heavenly Father,

Grant me the discernment to recognize the enemy's deceptions in my life. Open my eyes to see the truth and to avoid the snares set before me. Fill me with Your wisdom and understanding, and guide me in Your ways. Help me to stay vigilant and to seek Your guidance in all things. May Your truth be my foundation and Your word my light. Amen.

Prayer for Deliverance

Example Scenario: Emily feels oppressed by spiritual forces and seeks deliverance through prayer.

Prayer:

Loving God,

I feel oppressed by forces that seek to harm me spiritually. I ask for Your deliverance and protection. Break the chains that bind me and set me free from this oppression. Fill me with Your Holy Spirit and drive away any darkness from my life. Cover me with Your grace and peace, and restore my soul. In the name of Jesus, I claim victory over the enemy. Amen.

Prayer for Peace Amidst Spiritual Battles

Example Scenario: Michael is experiencing inner turmoil due to spiritual battles and seeks God's peace.

Prayer:

Dear Lord,

In the midst of spiritual battles, I seek Your peace. Calm the storm within me and fill my heart with Your tranquility. Help me to trust in Your protection and to rest in Your promises. May Your peace guard my heart and mind, and may Your presence bring me comfort. Strengthen my faith and remind me that You are with me always. Amen.

Prayer for Faith and Trust

Example Scenario: Linda's faith is wavering in the face of spiritual warfare, and she seeks to strengthen her trust in God.

Prayer:

Heavenly Father,

My faith feels weak in the face of spiritual warfare. Help me to trust in You completely and to stand firm in my faith. Strengthen my belief in Your power and goodness. Remind me of Your promises and Your faithfulness. May my faith be unshakeable, grounded in Your love and truth. I put my trust in You, knowing that You are my protector and my strength. Amen.

Prayer for Victory

Example Scenario: James is in the midst of a spiritual battle and seeks God's help to claim victory.

Prayer:

Almighty God,

I am in the midst of a spiritual battle, and I seek Your help to claim victory. Fill me with Your power and courage. Remind me that through Christ, I am more than a conqueror. Help me to stand firm in Your truth and to resist the enemy. Equip me with Your spiritual armor and guide me to victory. I trust in Your strength and Your promises. Amen.

Conclusion

Spiritual warfare requires us to be vigilant and steadfast in our faith. Through these prayers, we seek God's protection, strength, and guidance, confident in His promise to be our defender. May we stand firm in His truth, resist the enemy's schemes, and claim victory through the power of Jesus Christ.

Prayer

Heavenly Father,

We thank You for Your protection and guidance in our spiritual battles. As we lift up our prayers for spiritual warfare, we ask for Your strength, courage, and discernment. Help us to stand firm in our faith and to trust in Your power. May we find victory through Jesus Christ, our Lord and Savior. In Your holy name, we pray.

Amen.

PART VI
PRAYERS FOR
THE WORLD

PRAYERS FOR OUR TIME

CHAPTER 19
PRAYERS FOR NATIONS AND LEADERS

Let us offer prayers that uplift our nations and leaders.

Introduction

Praying for nations and leaders is crucial for fostering peace, justice, and prosperity across the globe. Through prayer, we can seek God's guidance, wisdom, and protection for those in positions of authority and for the well-being of all people. This chapter offers prayers for various aspects of national and international concerns, including prayers for wisdom, justice, peace, and unity. These prayers aim to uplift our leaders and nations, inviting God's transformative power into the governance and social fabric of our world.

Prayer for National Leaders

Example Scenario: Emma prays for her country's leaders, asking God to guide them in their decisions.

Prayer:

Heavenly Father,

I lift up our national leaders to You, asking for Your guidance and wisdom in their decisions. Grant them the courage to lead with integrity and compassion. May they seek justice and righteousness in all their actions. Help them to govern with humility and a genuine desire to serve the people. Fill their hearts with Your love and truth, and may Your will be done in our nation. Amen.

Prayer for Global Peace

Example Scenario: Mark prays for peace in conflict-ridden regions around the world.

Prayer:

Dear Lord,

I pray for peace in our world, especially in regions plagued by conflict and violence. Soften the hearts of those involved and bring about reconciliation and understanding. May Your peace, which surpasses all understanding, descend upon these areas and transform the lives of those affected. Guide the leaders and people towards peaceful resolutions and lasting harmony. Amen.

Prayer for Justice and Equality

Example Scenario: Rachel prays for justice and equality in her country and around the world.

Prayer:

Righteous God,

I pray for justice and equality in our nation and throughout the world. Help us to see and treat each other as equals, created in Your image. Guide our leaders to enact laws and policies that promote fairness and protect the rights of all people. May Your justice roll down like waters and righteousness like an ever-flowing stream. Help us to stand against injustice and to work towards a society that reflects Your love and equality. Amen.

Prayer for Wisdom in Governance

Example Scenario: John prays for local and national government officials to be granted wisdom in their governance.

Prayer:

Gracious God,

I ask for Your wisdom to be upon our government officials at every level. Grant them insight and understanding as they make decisions that affect the lives of many. Help them to seek Your guidance and to act with integrity and compassion. May their actions reflect Your justice and mercy, and may they lead with wisdom and discernment. Guide them to make choices that honor You and benefit all people. Amen.

Prayer for Unity and Healing

Example Scenario: Emily prays for unity and healing in her country, which is experiencing division and strife.

Prayer:

Loving God,

I pray for unity and healing in our nation. In times of division and strife, bring us together in Your love. Help us to listen to one another with open hearts and to seek common ground. Heal the wounds that divide us and restore relationships. May Your Spirit of peace and unity dwell among us, guiding us to work together for the common good. Amen.

Prayer for Economic Stability

Example Scenario: Michael prays for economic stability and provision for those struggling in his nation.

Prayer:

Heavenly Father,

I pray for economic stability and provision in our nation. Guide our leaders in creating policies that support sustainable growth and help those in need. Provide for those who are struggling and bless the work of their hands. May Your abundance flow through our communities, ensuring that everyone has access to the resources they need. Help us to be generous and to support one another in times of need. Amen.

Prayer for Environmental Stewardship

Example Scenario: Linda prays for leaders to make wise decisions regarding the environment and natural resources.

Prayer:

Creator God,

I pray for our leaders to make wise decisions regarding the environment and natural resources. Help them to see the importance of caring for Your creation and to take actions that protect and preserve it. Guide us all to be good stewards of the earth, ensuring that future generations can enjoy its beauty and resources. May we work together to find sustainable solutions and to honour You through our care for the environment. Amen.

Prayer for Courage and Integrity

Example Scenario: James prays for leaders to have the courage and integrity to make difficult but necessary decisions.

Prayer:

Gracious God,

I pray for our leaders to have the courage and integrity to make difficult but necessary decisions. Strengthen them to stand up for what is right, even when it is unpopular or challenging. Fill them with Your Spirit, guiding them to act with honesty and moral conviction. May their leadership inspire others to act with integrity and to seek the common good. Amen.

Conclusion

Praying for nations and leaders is a powerful way to invite God's presence and guidance into the governance of our world. Through these prayers, we seek wisdom, justice, peace, and unity for our leaders and nations. May God's transformative power bring about positive change, fostering a world that reflects His love and righteousness.

Prayer

Heavenly Father,

We thank You for the opportunity to lift up our nations and leaders in prayer. As we seek Your guidance and blessings, we ask for Your wisdom, peace, and justice to prevail. Help our leaders to act with integrity and compassion, and may Your will be done in our world. Guide us all to work together for the common good, reflecting Your love and grace in all we do. In Your holy name, we pray.

Amen.

CHAPTER 20
PRAYERS FOR THE CHURCH

Praying for the church is vital for its growth, unity, and effectiveness.

Introduction

The church, as the body of Christ, plays a crucial role in spreading the Gospel, fostering community, and serving as a beacon of hope and love. Praying for the church is vital for its growth, unity, and effectiveness in fulfilling God's mission. This chapter provides prayers for various aspects of the church's life and ministry, including prayers for unity, leadership, spiritual growth, and outreach. Through these prayers, we seek God's guidance, strength, and blessings for the church to flourish and fulfil its calling.

Prayer for Unity

Example Scenario: Emma prays for unity within her local church community, which has been experiencing divisions.

Prayer:

Heavenly Father,

I lift up our church community to You, asking for Your spirit of unity to dwell among us. Help us to put aside our differences and to come together in love and harmony. May we be one in Christ, reflecting Your love and grace to the world. Heal any divisions and strengthen our bonds of fellowship. Guide us to work together for Your kingdom, united in purpose and heart. Amen.

Prayer for Church Leaders

Example Scenario: Mark prays for the pastors, elders, and ministry leaders in his church.

Prayer:

Dear Lord,

I pray for our church leaders, including our pastors, elders, and ministry leaders. Grant them wisdom, strength, and guidance as they shepherd Your flock. Fill them with Your Holy Spirit and equip them to lead with integrity and compassion. May they be a source of encouragement and inspiration to the congregation. Protect them from burnout and discouragement, and bless their efforts in serving You. Amen.

Prayer for Spiritual Growth

Example Scenario: Rachel prays for the spiritual growth and maturity of the members of her church.

Prayer:

Gracious God,

I pray for the spiritual growth and maturity of our church members. Help us to deepen our relationship with You and to grow in our faith. May we hunger for Your word and seek to live according to Your will. Fill us with Your Holy Spirit and guide us in our spiritual journey. Strengthen our faith, and help us to support one another in our walk with You. Amen.

Prayer for Outreach and Evangelism

Example Scenario: John prays for his church's outreach and evangelism efforts to be effective and impactful.

Prayer:

Heavenly Father,

I lift up our church's outreach and evangelism efforts to You. Help us to be bold in sharing the Gospel and to reach out to those who do not know You. Give us compassion for the lost and the courage to proclaim Your truth. May our efforts be fruitful and bring many to a saving knowledge of Jesus Christ. Guide us to be a light in our community and to reflect Your love in all we do. Amen.

Prayer for Healing and Restoration

Example Scenario: Emily prays for healing and restoration within her church, which has been affected by recent challenges.

Prayer:

Loving God,

I pray for healing and restoration within our church. We have faced challenges that have left wounds and divisions. Pour out Your healing grace upon us and restore our fellowship. Help us to forgive one another and to seek reconciliation. May Your love bring healing to our hearts and unity to our community. Guide us to move forward with renewed hope and purpose. Amen.

Prayer for Discipleship and Mentorship

Example Scenario: Michael prays for effective discipleship and mentorship programs within his church.

Prayer:

Dear Lord,

I pray for our church's discipleship and mentorship programs. Help us to nurture and equip new believers in their faith. Guide us to create effective programs that foster spiritual growth and maturity. Raise up mentors who can guide and support others in their walk with You. May our church be a place where disciples are made and nurtured, growing in love and knowledge of You. Amen.

Prayer for Worship and Praise

Example Scenario: Linda prays for her church's worship services to be Spirit-filled and God-glorifying.

Prayer:

Heavenly Father,

I lift up our church's worship services to You. May our worship be filled with Your Spirit and bring glory to Your name. Help us to worship You in spirit and truth, with hearts fully devoted to You. Guide our worship leaders and musicians to lead us in songs of praise and adoration. May our worship draw us closer to You and inspire us to live for Your glory. Amen.

Prayer for Service and Mission

Example Scenario: James prays for his church's service and mission efforts to make a positive impact in the community and beyond.

Prayer:

Gracious God,

I pray for our church's service and mission efforts. Help us to be a beacon of hope and love in our community and beyond. Guide us to serve those in need with compassion and humility. Bless our mission trips and outreach programs, making them effective in spreading Your love and Gospel. May our church be known for its commitment to service and its impact on the world. Amen.

Conclusion

Praying for the church is essential for its growth, unity, and effectiveness in fulfilling God's mission. Through these prayers, we seek God's guidance, strength, and blessings for the church to flourish and fulfill its calling. May the church be a light in the world, reflecting God's love, grace, and truth.

Prayer

Heavenly Father,

We thank You for the gift of the church and the fellowship of believers. As we lift up our prayers for the church, we ask for Your guidance, strength, and blessings. Help us to grow in unity, to support our leaders, and to be effective in our mission to spread the Gospel. May Your love and grace fill our hearts and our church, drawing us closer to You and to one another. In Your holy name, we pray.

Amen.

CHAPTER 21
PRAYERS FOR
THE ENVIRONMENT

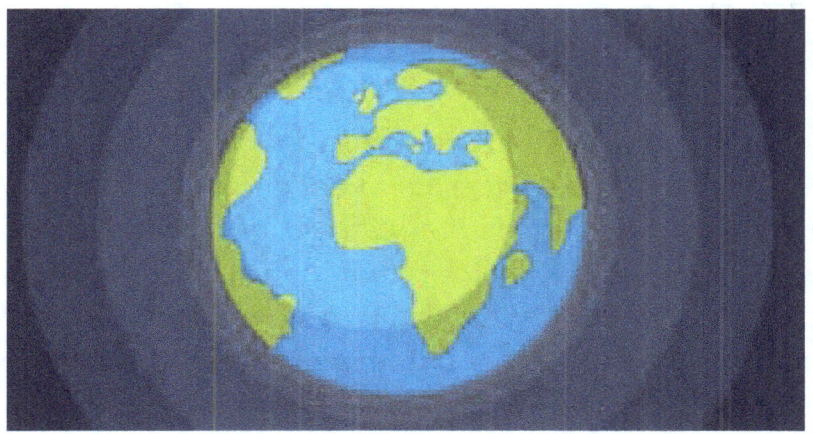

We are stewards of God's creation.

Introduction

Caring for the environment is an integral part of our responsibility as stewards of God's creation. Through prayer, we can seek God's guidance and blessing in our efforts to protect and restore the natural world. This chapter provides prayers for various aspects of environmental stewardship, including prayers for conservation, climate action, and appreciation of nature's beauty. These prayers aim to inspire and empower us to live sustainably and to honour God's creation in all we do.

Prayer for Environmental Stewardship

Example Scenario: Emma feels called to be more proactive in caring for the environment and seeks God's guidance in her efforts.

Prayer:

Creator God,

I come before You with a heart filled with gratitude for the beauty and wonder of Your creation. Guide me in my efforts to be a responsible steward of the environment. Help me to make choices that honor and protect the natural world. Give me wisdom and creativity in finding ways to reduce my environmental impact. May my actions reflect Your love for all of creation and inspire others to do the same. Amen.

Prayer for Conservation Efforts

Example Scenario: Mark is involved in local conservation efforts and prays for success and support for these initiatives.

Prayer:

Heavenly Father,

I lift up our local conservation efforts to You. Bless the work being done to protect and preserve our natural resources. Grant success to our initiatives and bring the support needed to continue this important work. Help us to be diligent and passionate in our efforts to care for the environment. May our conservation efforts bring about positive change and reflect Your glory. Amen.

Prayer for Climate Action

Example Scenario: Rachel is concerned about climate change and prays for effective action to address this global issue.

Prayer:

Gracious God,

I am deeply concerned about the impact of climate change on our planet. I pray for effective action to address this pressing issue. Guide our leaders and policymakers to make wise decisions that protect the environment and promote sustainability. Help us all to take meaningful steps to reduce our carbon footprint and to care for the earth. May we act with urgency and compassion, inspired by Your love for creation. Amen.

Prayer for the Healing of the Earth

Example Scenario: John prays for the healing and restoration of ecosystems damaged by human activity.

Prayer:

Loving God,

I pray for the healing and restoration of ecosystems that have been damaged by human activity. Bring renewal to areas affected by pollution, deforestation, and other forms of environmental degradation. Guide us to find sustainable solutions that promote the health and vitality of the earth. May Your healing touch restore the beauty and balance of creation. Amen.

Prayer for Appreciation of Nature

Example Scenario: Emily seeks to deepen her appreciation for the natural world and to cultivate a sense of wonder and gratitude.

Prayer:

Dear Lord,

I thank You for the beauty and majesty of the natural world. Help me to cultivate a deep appreciation for the environment and to see Your handiwork in all of creation. Fill my heart with wonder and gratitude for the gifts of nature. May this appreciation inspire me to protect and cherish the earth, honouring You through my actions. Amen.

Prayer for Sustainable Living

Example Scenario: Michael wants to adopt a more sustainable lifestyle and seeks God's guidance in making changes.

Prayer:

Heavenly Father,

I desire to live a more sustainable and eco-friendly life. Guide me in making changes that reduce my environmental impact and promote sustainability. Help me to be mindful of my consumption and to make choices that reflect my commitment to caring for the earth. May my lifestyle be a testimony to Your love for creation and inspire others to do the same. Amen.

Prayer for Environmental Justice

Example Scenario: Linda is concerned about the impact of environmental issues on marginalized communities and prays for justice.

Prayer:

God of Justice,

I lift up those who are disproportionately affected by environmental issues, especially marginalized communities. I pray for justice and equity in addressing these challenges. Help us to advocate for policies that protect the vulnerable and ensure that everyone has access to a healthy environment. May Your justice and mercy guide our actions and bring about positive change. Amen.

Prayer for Future Generations

Example Scenario: James prays for future generations to inherit a healthy and thriving planet.

Prayer:

Loving Creator,

I pray for future generations, that they may inherit a healthy and thriving planet. Help us to make decisions today that ensure the sustainability and well-being of the earth for those who come after us. Guide us to be faithful stewards of creation, leaving a legacy of care and respect *for the environment. May our efforts today pave the way for a brighter, greener future. Amen.*

Conclusion

Praying for the environment is a vital part of our role as stewards of God's creation. Through these prayers, we seek God's guidance, strength, and blessing in our efforts to protect and restore the natural world. May our actions reflect our love for creation and inspire others to join us in caring for the environment.

Prayer

Heavenly Father,

We thank You for the beauty and wonder of Your creation. As we lift up our prayers for the environment, we ask for Your guidance and blessing. Help us to be responsible stewards of the earth, making choices that honor and protect the natural world. May our efforts bring about positive change and reflect Your love for all of creation. In Your holy name, we pray.

Amen.

CHAPTER 22
PRAYERS FOR THE PERSECUTED

Prayer is the key to boldness and courage.

Introduction

Around the world, countless individuals face persecution for their faith. As members of the global body of Christ, it is our duty and privilege to lift up our persecuted brothers and sisters in prayer. This chapter offers prayers for strength, courage, protection, and hope for those who suffer for their faith. By praying for the persecuted, we seek God's intervention, comfort, and justice, standing in solidarity with those who endure hardship for the sake of the Gospel.

Prayer for Strength and Endurance

Example Scenario: Emma prays for Christians in countries where their faith is severely persecuted.

Prayer:

Heavenly Father,

I lift up my persecuted brothers and sisters around the world. Grant them the strength and endurance they need to withstand the trials they face. Fill them with Your Holy Spirit and empower them to remain steadfast in their faith. May Your presence bring them comfort and courage. Help them to hold on to Your promises and to find hope in Your unfailing love. Amen.

Prayer for Protection

Example Scenario: Mark prays for the safety and protection of persecuted Christians who are at risk of violence.

Prayer:

Dear Lord,

I pray for the safety and protection of those who are persecuted for their faith. Surround them with Your divine protection and keep them safe from harm. Hide them under the shadow of Your wings and shield them from their enemies. May Your angels watch over them and guard them in all their ways. Give them peace in the midst of danger, knowing that You are their refuge and strength. Amen.

Prayer for Courage and Boldness

Example Scenario: Rachel prays for persecuted Christians to have the courage and boldness to share the Gospel despite the risks.

Prayer:

Gracious God,

I pray for my persecuted brothers and sisters to have the courage and boldness to share the Gospel, even in the face of danger. Fill them with Your Holy Spirit and grant them the words to speak. Help them to be fearless in proclaiming Your truth and to shine Your light in the darkest places. May their testimony bring many to a saving knowledge of Jesus Christ. Strengthen their resolve and embolden their witness. Amen.

Prayer for Hope and Comfort

Example Scenario: John prays for persecuted Christians who are feeling hopeless and discouraged.

Prayer:

Loving Father,

I lift up those who are feeling hopeless and discouraged due to persecution. Pour out Your comfort and hope upon them. Remind them of Your promises and Your unfailing love. Help them to find peace and solace in Your presence. Encourage their hearts and renew their strength. May they find hope in the knowledge that You are with them and that You will never leave them nor forsake them. Amen.

Prayer for Families of the Persecuted

Example Scenario: Emily prays for the families of persecuted Christians who are also affected by their loved ones' suffering.

Prayer:

Dear Lord,

I pray for the families of those who are persecuted for their faith. Comfort them in their worry and fear. Provide for their needs and protect them from harm. Give them strength and courage as they support their loved ones. Help them to trust in Your provision and care. May Your peace fill their hearts and sustain them through difficult times. Amen.

Prayer for Justice

Example Scenario: Michael prays for justice for persecuted Christians and for the end of their suffering.

Prayer:

God of Justice,

I pray for justice for those who are persecuted for their faith. Bring an end to their suffering and deliver them from the hands of their oppressors. Raise up leaders and advocates who will stand up for their rights and bring about change. May Your justice prevail and Your righteousness shine forth. Strengthen the hearts of those who seek to defend the persecuted, and guide them in their efforts. Amen.

Prayer for Forgiveness and Reconciliation

Example Scenario: Linda prays for persecuted Christians to find the strength to forgive their persecutors and seek reconciliation.

Prayer:

Merciful God,

I pray for my persecuted brothers and sisters to find the strength to forgive their persecutors. Fill their hearts with Your love and grace. Help them to follow the example of Jesus, who forgave those who persecuted Him. May their forgiveness be a powerful testimony of Your love and bring about reconciliation and healing. Guide them in their interactions and grant them peace in their hearts. Amen.

Prayer for Faith and Trust

Example Scenario: James prays for persecuted Christians to maintain their faith and trust in God despite their suffering.

Prayer:

Heavenly Father,

I pray for those who are persecuted for their faith to maintain their trust in You. Strengthen their faith and remind them of Your faithfulness. Help them to cling to Your promises and to find hope in Your word. May their faith be unshakeable, even in the face of persecution.

Guide them in their journey and fill them with Your peace. Amen.

Conclusion

Praying for the persecuted is a vital expression of our solidarity and love for our brothers and sisters in Christ. Through these prayers, we seek God's intervention, comfort, and justice for those who suffer for their faith. May our prayers bring hope and strength to the persecuted, and may we be inspired to act on their behalf.

Prayer

Heavenly Father,

We thank You for the opportunity to lift up our persecuted brothers and sisters in prayer. As we seek Your intervention and comfort, we ask for Your strength, protection, and justice to prevail. Help us to stand in solidarity with the persecuted and to support them in any way we can. May Your love and grace fill their hearts and sustain them through their trials. In Your holy name, we pray.

Amen.

PART VII
PRAYERS FOR SPECIAL OCCASIONS

CHAPTER 23
PRAYERS FOR HOLIDAYS AND CELEBRATIONS

Prayers during holidays and celebrations enrich our experiences.

Introduction

Holidays and celebrations are special times that bring people together, allowing us to reflect on our blessings, express gratitude, and create lasting memories. Praying during these moments can enrich our experiences, bringing a deeper sense of joy, gratitude, and spiritual connection. This chapter offers prayers for various holidays and celebrations, including prayers for Thanksgiving, Christmas, Easter, birthdays, and other significant milestones. These prayers aim to invite God's presence and blessing into our festive moments, making them even more meaningful and joyous.

Prayer for Thanksgiving

Example Scenario: Emma gathers with her family for Thanksgiving dinner and offers a prayer of gratitude for their blessings.

Prayer:

Heavenly Father,

We come before You with hearts full of gratitude on this Thanksgiving Day. Thank You for the abundance of blessings You have bestowed upon us. For the gift of family and friends, for the food on our table, and for the love and joy we share, we give You thanks. Help us to remember those who are less fortunate and to extend our blessings to others. May our hearts always be filled with gratitude for Your goodness and grace. Amen.

Prayer for Christmas

Example Scenario: Mark and his family gather around the Christmas tree to celebrate the birth of Jesus and offer a prayer.

Prayer:

Dear Lord,

As we celebrate the birth of Jesus, we thank You for the greatest gift of all—Your Son, our Saviour. Fill our hearts with the joy and wonder of His coming. Help us to remember the true meaning of Christmas and to share His love with those around us. Bless our time together as we celebrate with family and friends. May the light of Christ shine brightly in our lives and bring peace and hope to the world. Amen.

Prayer for Easter

Example Scenario: Rachel joins her church community for an Easter service and offers a prayer to celebrate the resurrection of Jesus.

Prayer:

Gracious God,

On this glorious Easter morning, we rejoice in the resurrection of our Lord Jesus Christ. Thank You for the victory over sin and death that He achieved for us. Fill our hearts with the joy and hope of the resurrection. Help us to live as Easter people, sharing the good news of His resurrection with the world. May the promise of a new life in Christ inspire us to walk in faith and love. Amen.

Prayer for Birthdays

Example Scenario: John celebrates his birthday with friends and family and offers a prayer of thanks for another year of life.

Prayer:

Loving Father,

Thank You for the gift of another year of life. As I celebrate my birthday, I am grateful for Your faithfulness and love. Thank You for the blessings of family, friends, and the experiences that have shaped me. Guide me in the year ahead, helping me to grow in faith and to walk in Your ways. May my life be a reflection of Your grace and goodness. Bless this celebration and the people who share it with me. Amen.

Prayer for Anniversaries

Example Scenario: Emily and her spouse celebrate their wedding anniversary and offer a prayer of gratitude for their marriage.

Prayer:

Dear Lord,

We thank You for the gift of our marriage and for the years we have shared together. As we celebrate our anniversary, we are grateful for Your love and guidance. Strengthen our bond and help us to continue growing in love and commitment to each other. May our relationship be a reflection of Your love and grace. Bless our future together and help us to always seek You in our marriage. Amen.

Prayer for New Year's Day

Example Scenario: Michael gathers with friends to welcome the New Year and offers a prayer for blessings and guidance in the coming year.

Prayer:

Heavenly Father,

As we welcome the New Year, we thank You for the blessings of the past year and look forward to the opportunities ahead. Guide us with Your wisdom and grace in the coming year. Help us to seek Your will in all we do and to grow in faith and love. May this year be filled with joy, peace, and a deeper relationship with You. Bless our endeavours and help us to live out Your purpose for our lives. Amen.

Prayer for Graduations

Example Scenario: Linda attends her child's graduation ceremony and offers a prayer of gratitude and blessing for the future.

Prayer:

Gracious God,

We thank You for the accomplishments and hard work that have led to this graduation day. Bless the graduates as they embark on a new chapter in their lives. Guide them with Your wisdom and fill them with Your Spirit. Help them to use their gifts and talents to make a positive impact in the world. May they always seek Your guidance and trust in Your plans for their future. Amen.

Prayer for Weddings

Example Scenario: James attends a wedding and offers a prayer for the couple's future together.

Prayer:

Heavenly Father,

We lift up this couple to You as they begin their journey together in marriage. Bless their union and fill their hearts with love, patience, and understanding. Help them to build their relationship on the foundation of Your love and grace. Guide them through the joys and challenges of married life and strengthen their commitment to each other. May their marriage be a reflection of Your love and bring glory to Your name. Amen.

Conclusion

Praying during holidays and celebrations enhances our joy and deepens our connection with God. These prayers help us to express gratitude, seek blessings, and invite God's presence into our festive moments. May our celebrations be filled with joy, love, and a sense of God's abiding presence.

Prayer

Heavenly Father,

We thank You for the gift of holidays and celebrations that bring joy and togetherness into our lives. As we gather to celebrate these special moments, we ask for Your blessing and presence. Fill our hearts with gratitude, love, and a deeper connection to You. May our celebrations honour You and bring us closer to one another. In Your holy name, we pray.

Amen.

CHAPTER 24
PRAYERS FOR
LIFE MILESTONES

Through prayer, we express our gratitude to God for significant life milestones.

Introduction

Life is marked by various milestones that signify growth, achievement, and transition. These moments are opportunities for us to reflect on God's faithfulness, seek His guidance, and express our gratitude. This chapter provides prayers for significant life milestones such as births, graduations, weddings, and retirements. By turning to prayer during these pivotal moments, we invite God's presence and blessing, ensuring that our journeys are aligned with His will and filled with His grace.

Prayer for a Newborn Baby

Example Scenario: Emma and her family welcome a new baby into their lives and offer a prayer of thanksgiving and blessing.

Prayer:

Heavenly Father,

We thank You for the precious gift of this newborn baby. Bless this child with Your love, protection, and guidance. May Your presence be with them throughout their life, guiding them in Your ways. Grant wisdom and strength to the parents as they nurture and raise this child. Fill their home with joy, peace, and Your divine love. Amen.

Prayer for Starting School

Example Scenario: Mark prays for his child as they prepare to start their first day of school.

Prayer:

Dear Lord,

As my child begins their journey in school, I ask for Your blessing upon them. Help them to learn, grow, and thrive in this new environment. Grant them confidence, curiosity, and a love for learning. Protect them from harm and guide them in making good friends. May their school years be filled with joy and discovery, and may they always feel Your presence with them. Amen.

Prayer for Graduation

Example Scenario: Rachel prays for her friend who is graduating from college and starting a new chapter in their life.

Prayer:

Gracious God,

We celebrate this graduation day and the accomplishments it represents. Thank You for the hard work, dedication, and perseverance that have brought us to this moment. Bless the graduates as they step into the future. Guide their path and grant them wisdom in their decisions. May they use their talents and education to make a positive impact in the world. Fill their hearts with hope and courage as they embrace new opportunities. Amen.

Prayer for a New Job

Example Scenario: John prays for guidance and blessing as he starts a new job.

Prayer:

Loving Father,

I thank You for the opportunity to begin this new job. Guide me in my work and help me to use my skills and talents to serve others. Grant me wisdom, patience, and a positive attitude as I navigate this new environment. Bless my relationships with colleagues and superiors, and help me to be a light in the workplace. May this job be a source of fulfillment and growth, and may I honour You in all I do. Amen.

Prayer for Engagement

Example Scenario: Emily and her fiancé offer a prayer of gratitude and blessing as they prepare for marriage.

Prayer:

Dear Lord,

We thank You for bringing us together and for the love we share. As we prepare for marriage, bless our engagement and guide us in our journey together. Help us to build a strong foundation based on Your love and grace. Grant us patience, understanding, and joy as we plan for our future. May our relationship be a reflection of Your love and a testimony to Your goodness. Amen.

Prayer for Marriage

Example Scenario: Michael and his spouse offer a prayer on their wedding day, asking for God's blessing on their marriage.

Prayer:

Heavenly Father,

We stand before You on our wedding day, grateful for the love that has brought us together. Bless our marriage and fill our hearts with Your love. Help us to support and cherish each other, growing together in faith and commitment. Guide us through the joys and challenges of married life, and may our union be a reflection of Your grace and love. Bless our families and friends who support us, and may our home be filled with peace and joy. Amen.

Prayer for Parenthood

Example Scenario: Linda and her spouse pray for guidance and strength as they embark on the journey of parenthood.

Prayer:

Gracious God,

We thank You for the gift of parenthood and the blessing of children. Guide us as we raise our children, giving us wisdom, patience, and love. Help us to be good examples and to teach them Your ways. May our home be a place of safety, joy, and faith. Bless our children and help them to grow in knowledge, love, and grace. Strengthen our family bonds and help us to trust in Your guidance. Amen.

Prayer for Retirement

Example Scenario: James offers a prayer of gratitude and blessing as he retires from his career.

Prayer:

Heavenly Father,

I thank You for the years of work and the opportunities I have had in my career. As I enter this new phase of retirement, bless me with good health, peace, and fulfillment. Help me to find joy in new activities and to use my time in ways that honor You. Guide me in serving others and in deepening my relationship with You. May this season of life be filled with Your blessings and grace. Amen.

Prayer for Moving to a New Home

Example Scenario: Emma and her family pray for God's blessing as they move to a new home.

Prayer:

Dear Lord,

As we move to our new home, we ask for Your blessing and guidance. May this home be a place of safety, joy, and love. Help us to settle in quickly and to create a warm and welcoming environment. Bless our relationships with new neighbours and help us to be a light in our community. Guide us in this transition and fill our home with Your peace and presence. Amen.

Conclusion

Life milestones are significant moments that mark our journey and growth. Through prayer, we invite God's presence and blessing into these moments, seeking His guidance, strength, and grace. May our prayers enrich our experiences and help us to honour God in every stage of life.

Prayer

Heavenly Father,

We thank You for the milestones that mark our lives and for Your presence with us through every transition. As we celebrate and navigate these significant moments, we ask for Your blessing and guidance. Help us to honour You in all we do and to seek Your will in every step. May our lives be filled with Your grace, love, and peace. In Your holy name, we pray.

Amen.

CHAPTER 25
PRAYERS FOR DIFFICULT TIMES

By turning to God in prayer, we find solace in His presence.

Introduction

Life is filled with challenges and hardships that can test our faith and resilience. During these times, prayer becomes a vital source of strength, comfort, and guidance. This chapter offers prayers for various difficult situations, including illness, loss, anxiety, and financial struggles. By turning to God in prayer, we find solace in His presence, assurance in His promises, and hope for a brighter future.

Prayer for Strength in Illness

Example Scenario: Emma prays for her friend who is battling a serious illness.

Prayer:

Heavenly Father,

I lift up my friend who is struggling with illness. Grant them strength and courage to face each day. Surround them with Your healing presence and bring comfort to their body and spirit. Guide the hands of their medical team and provide them with wisdom and skill. May Your peace that surpasses all understanding guard their heart and mind. Help them to trust in Your love and to find hope in Your promises. Amen.

Prayer for Comfort in Loss

Example Scenario: Mark grieves the loss of a loved one and seeks God's comfort and peace.

Prayer:

Dear Lord,

In this time of deep sorrow, I turn to You for comfort and peace. My heart is heavy with grief, and I feel lost without my loved one. Wrap me in Your loving arms and help me to feel Your presence. Give me the strength to endure this pain and to find solace in Your promises of eternal life. May Your peace fill my heart, and may I find hope in the assurance that we will be reunited in Your presence. Amen.

Prayer for Peace in Anxiety

Example Scenario: Rachel is overwhelmed with anxiety about her future and prays for peace and clarity.

Prayer:

Gracious God,

I come before You with a heart full of anxiety and worry. The uncertainties of life feel overwhelming, and I struggle to find peace. Calm my restless spirit and fill me with Your peace. Help me to trust in Your plans and to surrender my fears to You. Guide me with Your wisdom and give me clarity in my decisions. May Your presence bring me comfort and assurance that You are in control. Amen.

Prayer for Guidance in Financial Struggles

Example Scenario: John faces financial difficulties and prays for God's provision and guidance.

Prayer:

Loving Father,

I am facing financial struggles that feel insurmountable. I turn to You for provision and guidance. Help me to manage my resources wisely and to find solutions to my financial problems. Provide for my needs and open doors of opportunity. Give me peace in the midst of uncertainty and help me to trust in Your faithfulness. May I find security in Your promises and strength in Your presence. Amen.

Prayer for Strength in Relationships

Example Scenario: Emily experiences difficulties in her marriage and prays for healing and reconciliation.

Prayer:

Dear Lord,

I lift up my marriage to You as we face struggles and conflicts. Help us to find healing and reconciliation. Give us the strength to forgive and to seek understanding. Guide us in rebuilding trust and restoring our relationship. Fill our hearts with Your love and grace, and help us to communicate with kindness and respect. May our marriage be a reflection of Your love and a testimony to Your faithfulness. Amen.

Prayer for Courage in Facing Challenges

Example Scenario: Michael is facing a difficult decision at work and prays for courage and wisdom.

Prayer:

Heavenly Father,

I am facing a challenging situation and feel uncertain about the right path to take. Grant me the courage to face this challenge with confidence and faith. Give me wisdom to make the right decisions and to act with integrity. Help me to trust in Your guidance and to rely on Your strength. May Your presence bring me peace and assurance as I navigate this difficult time. Amen.

Prayer for Patience in Waiting

Example Scenario: Linda waits for a breakthrough in her career and prays for patience and perseverance.

Prayer:

Gracious God,

Waiting is hard, and I feel discouraged as I wait for a breakthrough in my career. Grant me patience and perseverance to endure this season of waiting. Help me to trust in Your timing and to remain faithful in my efforts. Strengthen my resolve and keep me focused on Your promises. May I find hope and encouragement in Your presence and in the assurance that You are working all things for my good. Amen.

Prayer for Comfort in Loneliness

Example Scenario: James feels isolated and lonely and prays for God's comfort and companionship.

Prayer:

Loving Father,

I feel isolated and lonely, and my heart aches for companionship. Wrap me in Your loving embrace and help me to feel Your presence. Bring people into my life who will offer friendship and support. Fill my heart with Your peace and help me to find joy in Your presence. May I feel Your love surrounding me and find comfort in the assurance that You are always with me. Amen.

Prayer for Hope in Despair

Example Scenario: Emma feels hopeless about her future and prays for renewed hope and encouragement.

Prayer:

Heavenly Father,

I feel overwhelmed by despair and struggle to find hope for the future. Lift my spirit and fill me with Your hope. Help me to see beyond my current circumstances and to trust in Your plans for my life. Renew my strength and encourage my heart. May Your promises bring me comfort and hope, and may I find joy in the assurance that You are with me always. Amen.

Prayer for Strength in Faith

Example Scenario: Mark feels his faith wavering during a difficult time and prays for renewed strength and trust in God.

Prayer:

Dear Lord,

My faith feels weak, and I struggle to trust in Your goodness during this difficult time. Strengthen my faith and help me to trust in Your promises. Remind me of Your faithfulness and love. Fill my heart with Your peace and help me to rely on Your strength. May I find comfort and assurance in Your presence, and may my faith be renewed and strengthened. Amen.

Conclusion

Difficult times are a part of life, but through prayer, we can find strength, comfort, and hope in God's presence. These prayers offer a way to seek His guidance and assurance, reminding us that we are never alone in our struggles. May our faith be strengthened, and may we find peace in the knowledge that God is with us through every trial.

Prayer

Heavenly Father,

We thank You for Your constant presence and love, especially during difficult times. As we face challenges and hardships, we ask for Your strength, comfort, and guidance. Help us to trust in Your promises and to rely on Your grace. May Your peace fill our hearts and Your hope sustain us. In Your holy name, we pray.

Amen.

CHAPTER 26
THE TRANSFORMATIVE POWER OF PRAYER

making TIME for GOD

Prayer connects us with God and transforms our lives.

Introduction

Prayer is a profound and powerful practice that connects us to God, transforming our hearts, minds, and lives. Through prayer, we experience God's love, guidance, and peace, and we grow in our faith and understanding of His will. This final chapter explores the transformative power of prayer, highlighting how it can bring about personal change, deepen our relationship with God, and impact the world around us.

The Personal Transformation Through Prayer

Example Scenario: Emma reflects on how her daily prayers have transformed her attitude and outlook on life.

Reflection:

Heavenly Father,

As I look back on my journey of prayer, I see how You have transformed my heart and mind. Through daily conversations with You, I have found peace in the midst of chaos, hope in times of despair, and strength in moments of weakness. My attitudes and perspectives have shifted, and I now see the world through the lens of Your love and grace. Thank You for the transformative power of prayer that has renewed my spirit and drawn me closer to You. Amen.

Deepening Our Relationship with God

Example Scenario: Mark shares how prayer has deepened his relationship with God and strengthened his faith.

Reflection:

Dear Lord,

Through prayer, I have come to know You more intimately. Each moment spent in Your presence has deepened my understanding of Your character and love. I have learned to trust You more fully and to seek Your will in all areas of my life. My faith has grown stronger, and my connection to You has become a source of unwavering strength and comfort. Thank You for the gift of prayer that has brought me closer to You and enriched my spiritual journey. Amen.

The Impact of Intercessory Prayer

Example Scenario: Rachel discusses the power of praying for others and witnessing the impact of those prayers.

Reflection:

Gracious God,

Interceding for others in prayer has shown me the power of Your love and mercy. As I have lifted up friends, family, and even strangers to You, I have seen Your hand at work in their lives. Miracles of healing, reconciliation, and provision have testified to Your goodness and faithfulness. Thank You for the privilege of partnering with You through intercessory prayer and for the ways it has impacted the lives of those I care about. Amen.

Prayer as a Source of Guidance and Wisdom

Example Scenario: John recounts how seeking God's guidance in prayer has led him to wise decisions and fruitful paths.

Reflection:

Loving Father,

In times of uncertainty, I have sought Your guidance through prayer and found wisdom beyond my understanding. Your Spirit has led me to make decisions that align with Your will and have brought about fruitful outcomes. Thank You for the clarity and direction that prayer provides, and for the assurance that You are guiding my steps. May I continue to seek Your wisdom in all areas of my life. Amen.

The Healing Power of Prayer

Example Scenario: Emily shares how prayer has brought emotional and physical healing in her life.

Reflection:

Dear Lord,

Prayer has been a source of healing for my body, mind, and spirit. In times of pain and distress, I have cried out to You and found comfort and restoration. Your healing touch has mended my wounds and brought peace to my troubled heart. Thank You for the transformative power of prayer that heals and renews. May I always turn to You in times of need, trusting in Your unfailing love. Amen.

Prayer as a Catalyst for Change

Example Scenario: Michael talks about how prayer has been a catalyst for positive change in his community.

Reflection:

Heavenly Father,

Through prayer, I have witnessed the power of Your Spirit to bring about positive change in my community. Prayers for justice, peace, and unity have resulted in tangible actions and transformations. Thank You for using prayer as a catalyst for change, and for the ways it mobilizes us to act according to Your will. May we continue to pray fervently for our communities and work towards a better world. Amen.

Conclusion

The transformative power of prayer is evident in every aspect of our lives. Through personal transformation, deepened relationships with God, intercessory prayers, guidance, healing, and community impact, we see the profound ways in which prayer changes us and the world around us. As we conclude this book, let us embrace the power of prayer, committing to a life of continual conversation with our Creator. May our prayers be a source of strength, hope, and transformation, drawing us ever closer to the heart of God.

Prayer

Heavenly Father,

We thank You for the gift of prayer and the ways it transforms our lives. As we conclude this journey through prayer, we ask for Your continued guidance and presence in our lives. Help us to remain faithful in our prayers, seeking You in all circumstances. May our lives be a testament to the transformative power of prayer, and may we draw others to You through our example. Fill our hearts with Your love, peace, and grace, and help us to live each day in the light of Your presence. In Your holy name, we pray.

Amen.

PRAYERS FOR OUR TIME

CLOSING PRAYER

Heavenly Father,

As we conclude this journey of reflection and prayer, we come before You with hearts full of gratitude. Thank You for the countless ways You have guided us, comforted us, and drawn us closer to You through these prayers. We are grateful for Your unwavering presence in our lives, especially in times of joy, sorrow, hope, and struggle.

Lord, we ask that You continue to walk with us, guiding our steps and illuminating our paths. Help us to carry the lessons we have learned and the prayers we have offered into our daily lives. May our hearts remain open to Your voice, and may our spirits be ever willing to follow Your will.

Bless us with the courage to face challenges with faith, the wisdom to seek Your guidance, and the compassion to extend Your love to those around us. Let our lives be a reflection of Your grace and mercy, and may we be instruments of Your peace in a world that so desperately needs it.

As we move forward, may we always remember the transformative power of prayer. Strengthen our commitment to daily conversation with You, and help us to trust in Your promises. Fill us with hope, renew our spirits, and lead us in Your everlasting ways.

Thank You, Lord, for Your infinite love and faithfulness. May our prayers continue to rise to You, and may we find comfort and strength in Your presence. In Your holy and precious name, we pray.

Amen.

*With this final prayer, we seal our journey of **"Prayers for Our Time,"** trusting that God's hand will continue to guide and bless each of us as we walk in faith and love.*

www.ingramcontent.com/pod-product-compliance
Lightning Source LLC
Chambersburg PA
CBHW070549010526
44118CB00012B/1271